Food for l

D1650515

Food for life

Personal Bible study
made appetizing

Peter Lee, Greg Scharf
and Robert Willcox

'Ignorance of Scripture is ignorance
of Christ'—*Jerome*

Inter-Varsity Press

INTER-VARSITY PRESS

38 De Montfort Street, Leicester LE1 7GP, England

First published 1977
Reprinted 1978

ISBN 0 85110 397 9

Text set in 10pt Photon Univers,
printed by photolithography,
and bound in Great Britain at
The Pitman Press, Bath

Inter-Varsity Press is the publishing division of
the Universities and Colleges Christian Fellowship
(formerly the Inter-Varsity Fellowship), a student
movement linking Christian Unions in universities
and colleges throughout the British Isles, and a
member movement of the International Fellowship of
Evangelical Students. For information about local
and national activities in Great Britain write
to UCCF, 38 De Montfort Street, Leicester LE1 7GP.

Acknowledgments

At the time of writing we were all serving churches in central London; Peter Lee at St Paul's, Onslow Square; Greg Scharf at All Souls, Langham Place; and Robert Willcox at St Helen's, Bishopsgate. Our thanks are due primarily to those churches for what they taught us, for looking at some of the material in manuscript form, and for tolerating our spending time on *Food for life*. Much of our secretarial help came from those churches, and we should like especially to thank Jan Cash, Barbara Emberson, Eileen Adby and Lesley Parsons.

In particular we should like to thank Raymond Turvey, Michael Baughen and Dick Lucas, vicar and rectors respectively of the above churches, for letting us do the job. We thank them too, along with many other Christian teachers, for the scholarship they have gathered from others over the years and made available in public or private so that we could learn and recycle it in the book.

Peter's wife and child have been magnificent in their tolerance. During the writing stage Greg acquired a fiancée and married her – somehow! – and is grateful for her long-suffering. Robert thanks colleagues and friends for their patience.

Contents

1
Introduction

Why study the Bible?

Life and food are both God-given. Maybe that is why Jesus often used the metaphor of food and drink to speak of the fulfilment God provides at deeper levels than those of bodily hunger and thirst. He bluntly called himself the bread of life, and was bold enough to add that whoever comes to him will not hunger, and whoever trusts in him will never thirst again. More broadly, he presented the whole of God's truth and the desire to obey it as the food which truly feeds. He said that man cannot live by bread only, but that he must live by the words of God. His own food, he said, was to do the will of God. The Bible in many places picks up the analogy and speaks of itself, second to Christ, as everyone's *food for life*. This book, therefore, is written in the hope that it will help those Christians who want to get to grips with studying the Bible. We use the metaphor of feeding because that is the Bible's own picture for nourishing oneself on God's truth; and we offer a choice of diets which you can sample according to your level of knowledge and Christian maturity.

Of course the whole idea may make no sense to you at all. If, for example, you have just picked this book up in a friend's flat, and you claim no kind of Christian allegiance yourself, the very idea of using the Bible for strength and guidance may seem silly. You perhaps think that the Bible is of interest as history, like many other documents; and that it contains beauty and wisdom, like much other literature; but no more. Christians would want to push the thing much further than this, though, and say that Christianity is not just a system of ideas or morals, but at heart a relationship between a living God and human beings for whom he cares. In this the Bible is a line of communication, much more like letters from a friend than anything else. Prayer too makes sense, if such a living relationship is a reality. If you find that an attractive or intriguing thought, you may be wise to tackle your Christian friend and find out more; or you could look at the early studies in this book and see if the Bible can speak for itself.

Because Christianity is a relationship, many Christians try to make a regular space in their lives for listening to the Bible and soaking themselves in its implications. Like any relationship worth the name, our love for God needs time and attention. This kind of opportunity for study, thought and prayer (sometimes called a 'quiet time') is an ideal way of giving both. God can reach us as we read his letters; we can reach him as we pray about our lives and what we have learnt. Although (as in every friendship) there are times when it seems routine, the long-term effect will be one of deepening trust and understanding. It is sad to see people who have begun a relationship with Christ and then neglect it, as if they had 'arrived'. The New Testament envisages not only converts, but people who are mature in their knowledge of God. Besides, we live in a world whose regular and systematic influence tends to resist our Christian progress; we need to give God the chance to advance it by his influence the other way. To stand still is to slide backwards.

Unfortunately, even some Christians are unsure about the value of the Bible; they have heard that they should read it, but they have never really seen why. But if the Bible is a set of letters from a friend who created the universe, died on the cross, and lives to rule the world for ever, it becomes rather an exciting book! This is just what Christians claim: that God stirred the writers of the Bible to carry his truth to human beings through history, poetry, letters and song, in a way that would bring unchanging truth with daily freshness to those who love him. For the Christian who wants to grow, this chance to explore God's truth is valuable enough. But God has gone farther and made the Bible both enjoyable and highly practical. He has given us examples to follow, dangers to avoid, and warnings of where trouble lies. Through the Bible he portrays the character of Christ, which shows up the bad in our own lives and helps us to change in his direction. In the Bible, too, he gives us guidelines for dealing with personal and social problems, and for planning our own futures.

Where to start

Supposing, then, that you want all this: what do you do? How do you set about finding what God wants to say to you today?

The first thing you need is a Bible. Get one you can un-

11

derstand, in a fresh but accurate version. There are no end of modern versions around, and it may be wise to buy one that your Christian friends use, so that you can study it together. The Revised Standard Version is largely accurate and still widely used; the New English Bible is more modern and a bit more precise, but can be stilted. The Living Bible is an excellent paraphrase but does not pretend to be accurate enough for careful study; the Jerusalem Bible, despite eccentricities, is also good. The New International Version offers accuracy and readability. The Good News Bible is an excellent translation in everyday language, and is sufficiently similar to the RSV (which we have used for this book) to make its use with *Food for life* quite straightforward. Both the style and precision of the Authorised Version are really too antiquated for today; so, probably, is whatever blotty school-issue Bible you possess, with all the homework in the margins! Buy a Bible as up-to-date as your faith, and be prepared to spend some money on one you will treasure.

The next thing you need to do is to work out a place and time where you can be quiet and uninterrupted. For many people—even students— this has to be first thing in the morning or last thing at night, or it never happens. Fairly early in the day has one big advantage—the bulk of the day is still in front of you, with all its opportunities for putting into practice what you have learnt!

When you are settled and ready to start, pray; ask God to help you understand the passage, both its general truth and any particular application to yourself. Having chosen your passage of the Bible to study (more on this below), read it straight through, to see the over-all picture and the main message; if possible read a bit before and after it to get it in context. Then read the passage a second time, looking for significant detail, special points of interest or problems. Take time to think through the second reading; spot the main truths taught about God (Father, Son and Spirit), about man, the world, the future, *etc.* Notice facts. See where the passage is relevant in your own life—anything clearly to do or follow, to watch or avoid. Always ask what the passage *says*, what it *means*, and *how it applies*. Then jot down the main things you have learnt; this will focus them, as well as form a record. Use a loose-leaf notebook for this; then you can keep your notes in a logical order. At this stage—not before—read any notes you may be using, from this book or any study guide you are on. These should provide factual help, fresh ideas and thoughtful questions. But *don't* read them sooner, or they may dominate your own thinking which should be based on the text itself. Add any more jottings resulting from the notes; if there is time, you may like to re-read the passage rapidly to fix it in your mind.

Now pray over your findings, thanking God for truth or encouragement, facing any challenges, asking for a changed life and renewed service for him along any lines the passage suggests. Then you may like to widen the focus and pray more generally over any Christian commitments you have—family, friends, work, church life or the wider world and its needs.

This procedure may seem formidable; but please remember that in this full form it is something of an ideal, and most people will not follow all of it on every occasion. Try to get the over-all picture most times, and more when you can. To begin with, ten or fifteen minutes will be plenty, growing to half an hour or more as time goes on. For easy reference you will find the sequence of suggestions above summarized in the first section of studies, on page 18. If you are not sure where to start in the Bible study, then we suggest that you follow the studies in that section, which are designed to cover the main elements of Christian belief and behaviour, and to introduce you to some fundamental passages of Scripture and the means of studying them.

Learning in fellowship

It should be said that this individual study which has been discussed, vital as it is, is insufficient by itself. At the very least we need to be hearing biblical teaching in the local Christian church to which we belong. It is part of our pastor's responsibility to give clear and relevant explanations of Christian truth which affect our own lives and that of the whole fellowship. We should put ourselves under the authority of such teaching, not accepting everything uncritically but making sure that we are present regularly and are taught systematically. Many people also find some intermediate level of learning helpful—a group Bible study (see p. 163) or a training course of some kind. The aim is not knowledge for its own sake, but learning with a view to greater personal maturity in Christ and greater effectiveness in his service.

Prayer

Something similar applies to prayer. In a way it is, of course, an individual affair; it is closely allied with Bible study for the obvious reason that communication *from* God provokes communication *to* him. It is a kind of conversation in which we can talk over the points raised in his letter. As such it will involve all the usual aspects of conversation—expressing our appreciation, sharing joy, saying sorry, asking for help, thrashing through problems, and so on. Then it is an easy transition to the wider kind of praying mentioned above, when we can bring into the conversation the people and problems around us and ask the Lord for his involvement, guidance and help in them. Of course initially these concerns may be few and fairly local; but as our Christian responsibilities grow and our interests expand, they may become quite extensive. There may come a time when some kind of list is the only way to remember all the people we want to pray for. As with Bible study, a little planning and common sense go a long way.

Praying, like Bible study, also has its corporate aspect, in which it is helpful and right to be involved. There will be some praying publicly when your whole fellowship meets, but this is where the small group really comes into its own. When a few people really know each other and have given time to studying God's Word in the Bible together, they can often share their needs and concerns very freely. Then a time of prayer in which people can simply ask God to help with one another's problems—not to mention thanking him for their joys—becomes one of the richest Christian experiences.

Problems

So far so good. But how about the person who knows all this, and has practised it for years, but is now frankly stuck? Bible study so easily becomes a routine, a heavy and boring duty, rather than a journey of discovery. There can be all kinds of reasons for this. For some there may be an underlying spiritual problem of disobedience or rebellion against God over some issue, and nothing will ever come right until this is resolved. For others a visit to their pastor for counselling may be needed. For all of us there has to be the realization that the newness of the first days of Christian living cannot (by definition) last for ever. As in a marriage, there comes a settled relationship which may have fewer fireworks than before, but is more mature, deep and satisfying than in the early days.

The place of this book

For many people, though, the problem is quite a simple one; their *method* of Bible study has become dull, stereotyped, and repetitive. Perhaps they were shown one method, or put on to one system of readings when they first became a Christian. This was excellent then, but they may have outgrown it and now need something else. It is part of the aim of this book to help such people.

In Part II we have deliberately begun with basic studies for the new Christian. These will introduce him to the heart of the gospel, to the story of Jesus, and to the elements of Christian living. We envisage that these will be used at the rate of one a day, and we give a fair amount of explanation with some questions, prayers, verses to learn, and thoughts on how to apply the passages to our lives.

In fairness, it must be said that Food for life *aims to help you study the Bible for yourself; if you try to make our notes short-cut your study, you will not get much out of it.*

In Part III we branch out a bit and try to give examples of the various ways of approaching Bible study. These will cover new areas of the Bible as well as showing different approaches. While this book can be used straight through, you may find that you want to branch out on your own initiative at this stage; for instance, if one particular kind of study (say character studies) is being helpful, then visit your Christian bookshop and find some more materials of the same kind. Come back to this book later for something different if you want. Part IV goes a step further and tries to point to some more mature and stretching study. By then you may find the timetable changing so that you take more than one section a day, or so that you slow right down to look at a subject in depth.

Staleness can develop through always sticking to favourite passages, through always using one method, or through knowing only fragments of Scripture and missing the whole thrilling sweep of its message. Part of our attempt at a remedy has been to include pages on general subjects related to the Bible and Bible study, such as the unity of Scripture, memorization, or using a concordance (a what? See p. 125). As well as offering useful tips these should help you to produce your own tailor-made study plans in future.

If you use *Food for life* consecutively, it should last you about a year; it was written with that in mind. In that time you would cover a fair amount of the Bible. But don't let it bind you any more than any other system: it is not offered as a prescribed diet for all conditions, but as a kind of larder to turn to when you need it.

II
Milk:

a way in to
basic Bible study

In several places the New Testament refers to a new Christian as a newly born child, and to his food as milk. The suggestion is that his growth in Christ will be nourished by the basic elements of the Christian message. This first section of study therefore falls into three parts; it begins by trying to guide the very new Christian through *the heart of the gospel*, then explores *the Jesus story* and its significance, then looks at several *aspects of Christian living*. The idea is to learn a little about how to read the Bible for yourself, applying its message to your life and drawing close to God through study and prayer, as well as learning what these passages teach. If you are a very new Christian, or fancy a little revision, then we do suggest that you try to follow the studies in order; if not, you may prefer to skip this section and go on to Part III.

What to do in a time of Bible study and prayer

(Suggestions summarized from the introduction, for easy reference.)

Before you start:

1 Acquire an accurate but comprehensible version of the Bible
2 Work out a place and time where you can be quiet and uninterrupted

Then:

3 Pray that you will understand the chosen passage
4 Read it through once for general meaning
5 Read through carefully for detail, points of interest, problems
6 Think it through; spot the main truths and how they apply to yourself
7 Write down the main lessons to focus them and form a record
8 Read the notes for factual help or fresh ideas; jot down anything valuable
9 Pray over your findings, thanking God and asking for strength to practise what you have learnt
10 Pray more widely about your Christian commitments—family, work, worldwide

O God, help me to see what the Bible is saying, what it means, and how it applies to my life today.

1. The heart of the gospel

The gospel is not a formula. If it were, it could be summarized and mastered, and then we could all go on to greater and deeper things. Instead, the gospel is the great news that God has become man, and that that man, Jesus, is the Way, the Truth and the Life. He does not point to a pathway to life but invites us to know himself and thereby to know God. The gospel is the great news that sins are forgiven and that those who put their trust in Jesus have eternal life. It's that simple and yet it's not that simple. This is why the heart of the gospel is large—because at the heart of the gospel is Jesus. Jesus, explaining himself and being misunderstood and rejected. Jesus, showing us God and pressing God's invitation. Jesus, loving men and women as they were but also for what they could be. Jesus, meeting real needs. Jesus, being completely human yet totally divine. But Jesus doesn't do all the talking. His followers continued the explanation, recording their Master's words but also explaining the new life which he gave them. Even they don't make it simple for us! But they put into words great truths about Jesus and what it means to know and follow him.

It won't take long for you to realize that one secret in effective Bible study is learning to ask the right questions. For the next few weeks as you explore the heart of the gospel, ask the Bible questions about Jesus. Why did he come here? Why did he die? Who needs him? What does he want me to do? Jesus is the focal point of the whole Bible and we need to look for pointers to him on every page—even of the Old Testament. That's why we have included a few psalms at the end of this section. Not because they mention Jesus specifically, but because they teach truths which he came to unlock. We shall never know all there is to know about Jesus and the gospel, but we can all know enough to know God and to be personally known by him. That's why we start here. We pray that we won't stop.

(Read Romans 11:33–36)

Jesus talks about God   Mark 12 : 28–34

Jesus had just accused some of the religious leaders of not really knowing the power of God (24). Now another man, an expert in the Old Testament, asks a question which gives Jesus a chance to say something very significant about God. What kind of God could possibly demand what is required by those two commandments? How would things be different if there were more than one God? At first glance, it may seem that loving God totally would leave us with no love left for our neighbour. In fact it is only when we respond to God's love for us by obedience (the expression of our love for him) that we are able to love other people in the same way as we love ourselves. Memorizing Scripture is one method of growing in loving God with our minds. Try to memorize verses 29 and 30.

Jesus describes God's love   Luke 20 : 9–18

A parable is generally an imaginary story purposely designed by the teller to communicate one main point. Usually the characters of the parable are like the hearers, or God, or Jesus, in a particular respect. How is the owner of the vineyard like God? Why does God keep seeking sinful people? By rejecting the beloved son the tenants lost not only the privilege of working in the vineyard, they lost their lives as well. What does that statement, together with verse 18, have to say to the person who imagines that continuing to reject Jesus as Lord will have no effect on his life?

Father, thank you that you gave the life of your only Son that we might live. Thank you that one day even those who hate him will have to admit that he is Lord of all.

Jesus speaks out   Mark 1 : 21–34

Every Jewish community with at least ten families had a synagogue. There the scribes (supposed experts in the Old Testament and other Jewish writings designed to explain it) taught the people by quoting these books as authorities. Notice the impact that Jesus made. How was he different? Notice the word 'authority' in this passage. By comparing the different ways in which Jesus exercises authority, see if you can formulate a working definition of the word. Were

20

the demons right in their evaluation of who Jesus was and what he came to do (24)? From verse 31, could you infer anything about why Jesus heals people?

If you have time to pursue this important issue of authority, go on to read chapter 2:1–12. Does it tell you any more about where Jesus gets authority?

Jesus speaks to the tax man   Luke 19:1–10

From the reaction of Zacchaeus, what can we discover about public reaction to Jesus? Tax collectors had a bad reputation, partly because they were traitors representing the Roman oppressors and partly because more often than not they were dishonest, taking more tax than Rome required and pocketing the difference. Jesus may have heard of Zacchaeus or perhaps he just sensed his need. What did the bystanders mean when they complained (7)? Would they have used that word of themselves? What about Zacchaeus; did he consider himself to be a sinner? How do you know? From a human point of view, Zacchaeus was saved because he turned away from sin (repentance) and began to follow Jesus (first by making restitution). Does verse 10 help you to see what happened from a divine point of view?

Spend a few minutes tracing how God, 'the Hound of Heaven', sought you, exposed your lostness and saved you.

Jesus talks about the person God accepts
    Luke 18:9–14

In Jesus' day the Pharisees were a separatist sect within Judaism. They laid great stress on external righteousness, especially on avoiding evil company and keeping the fine points of the law. 'Tax collector' was synonymous with 'sinner' as far as Jesus' hearers were concerned. In what ways did the Pharisee's self-righteousness show up in his estimate of himself? In his attitude to God? In his attitude toward others? Contrast him with the tax collector. Which man was more realistic about himself and the nature of God? Notice the words used to describe how God answers the tax collector's prayer. The reason given (14) is significant.

All of us have within ourselves something of the Pharisee.

Ask God to show you where you have put your trust in yourself rather than in him.

Jesus explains our problems · Matthew 15:1–20

The Pharisees believed that eating food without having washed left a person ceremonially defiled. Where did Jesus locate the source of pollution? When speaking metaphorically, different cultures seem to associate certain actions or emotions with different parts of the body. We link the heart with emotions, the head with thoughts and the bowels (or 'guts') with determination. For the Jews and for Jesus the heart included what we would call the mind, the emotions, and the will. Jesus gives two reasons for the wrong conduct of the Pharisees (6 and 8). Which is the result of the other? The question is, if our hearts are the source of all those evil things (19), what can be done for us? Look up Romans 2:29 (which speaks of God's radical heart surgery) and Romans 10:8–11 (which reminds us of our part).

Jesus talks about himself · John 14:1–11

At the end of Jesus' earthly mission, just before his crucifixion, the apostles (the original twelve messengers) were understandably distraught when they learnt that Jesus must die and one of them would betray him. This passage contains the repeated assurance that to know Jesus is to know God—the God whose purposes cannot be thwarted. Pick out the statements which could only be made by someone equal with God. If we want to know more about God, where should we look (6, 9, 10)? Is there any provision for those who are not prepared simply to take Jesus' word? What does Jesus say was his purpose in going away?

Jesus told his followers that they knew a great deal about God already because they knew his only Son. Turn over in your mind the qualities of God which you already know through Jesus.

Jesus talks about his role · Luke 4:14–24

When Jesus returned to his home town he took the opportunity, when called upon to read in the synagogue, to apply to himself this part of Isaiah's prophecy. In your own words, summarize who Jesus is claiming to be and what he has come to do. Why did his neighbours have trouble believing him? If Jesus was wrong in claiming to be the man described by Isaiah, what should we conclude about him? What evidence is there that he was right?

Notice that Jesus customarily (16) attended synagogue, and must have been very familiar with the Old Testament to find this particular part when there were no chapter or verse numbers. What lesson is there for us who look to Jesus as our model as well as our teacher and Lord?

Jesus talks about his work   Mark 8:27—9:1

Peter, one of the more vocal of Jesus' followers, understood clearly who Jesus was, but had a hard time accepting what that meant. What were Peter's two sources of information? (See the parallel passage, Matthew 16:17, and Mark 8:33.) Following Jesus even to death is, paradoxically, the way to life. Satan tried to keep Jesus from the cross and he tries to keep us from following in Jesus' footsteps. From verses 35–38, what attractive alternatives to self-sacrificial living do you think the Evil One is likely to put forward?

Martin Luther once said, 'I have held many things in my hands and lost them all, but whatever I place in God's hands, that I always possess.'

Jesus interprets the law   Matthew 5:17–48

This passage, part of the Sermon on the Mount, tells us how the teaching of Jesus completes, extends and perfects the Old Testament. The key to understanding it is to realize that Jesus was preaching to separatists who were using the Old Testament to excuse their own sins and justify their behaviour. Jesus' teaching clarifies and reiterates the holy standards of a holy God. Notice Jesus' comment on the trustworthiness of the Old Testament and the danger of tampering with it. See if you can determine some of the ways those Jews misapplied or altered the intention of earlier commandments.

Although every word of Scripture is true, it must be understood in its wider context. In that light, how would you apply verses 29 and 30 to your life?

Principles of interpretation

To many people interpretation sounds like the art of making the Bible say whatever you want it to say. Interpreting the Bible is no different from trying to understand any other literature. The author uses words to convey ideas. The reader tries to understand exactly what the author wants to convey. This is true whether the author uses precise terms to make specific statements, or whether he uses language flexibly or poetically to suggest various levels of meaning. The science of interpretation follows orderly rules; not because following rules in itself will tell us all God wants us to learn from Scripture, but because if we disregard the rules of language we cannot be sure we have heard the truth God intended, however 'blessed' we may feel. Here are some rules of thumb:

1 Put yourself in the shoes of the author. Try to discover what the words meant to him, and what were his cultural background, historical situation, and readership. Look for themes and thoughts which he repeats; these will show his real concerns.

2 Approach Scripture empty-handed, not trying to make it say what you want.

3 Take the plain, ordinary sense of the passage unless there is a clear reason not to. If it calls Jesus *the Son of God*, that is that; if it calls him *the Lamb of God*, it suggests a sacrifice for sin, not a woolly quadruped.

4 Understand each word, verse, paragraph and book in its larger context. As in conversation, the parts contribute to a whole message; if a passage appears not to fit, we may have misunderstood it.

5 Understand less clear passages in the light of the clearer ones. Scripture is clear in many places about the fact that we are justified by faith and not by works; so when James says 'man is justified by works and not by faith alone', he is not contradicting the rest of the Bible, but saying that real faith leads to action.

6 Avoid applying any passage of Scripture to your life until you understand what it says.

Jesus explains the Old Testament   Luke 24 : 13–35
Jesus used his post-resurrection appearances to teach several truths. What is the most obvious one underlying this passage? What does Jesus have to say about himself and about the Old Testament? Notice the emotional state of Cleopas and his companion when they first met Jesus, and look at verse 21 for the reason. How did all that change as they listened to Jesus?

Today no-one sees Jesus physically, but he still has the power and desire to open our eyes to see who he is.

In verse 26, Jesus underscores the necessity of his suffering. Probably Isaiah 53 was among the passages he expounded to them. Read it through, and ask God to help you see how Jesus is foreshadowed there.

Jesus wins a loser   John 4 : 7–26
Jesus is speaking to someone who is both a Samaritan (a half breed despised by the Jews) and a woman (orthodox Jews would not speak to women in public). What does that say about Jesus? The Lord makes several important claims as he talks to the woman. Locate and mark them in your Bible so that you can use this passage later to explain to someone else just who Jesus claimed to be. What did the woman do when Jesus exposed the sinfulness of her lifestyle?

All of us need to face up to who Jesus is and who we are. As long as we think ourselves self sufficient, we will not turn to Jesus; but when we admit our need, Jesus forgives us and comes to live in us by his Spirit (14; *cf.* 7:38, 39).

Peter speaks about Jesus   Acts 2 : 22–24, 32–42
These verses record the very first Christian sermon and tell what happened when it was preached. What is Peter's subject? According to verses 23 and 24, was the resurrection unexpected? Peter wanted to convince his hearers of who Jesus was. Who does God say Jesus is (36)?

The response was dramatic because the Jews could not deny that Peter spoke the truth about Jesus and about themselves. What was the way out which Peter prescribed?

Meditate for a few minutes on what God did in Jesus to

provide salvation. Now think about what we must do to accept it.

Peter writes about Jesus 1 Peter 1 : 1–12

Peter is worshipping God for giving us such a salvation, and explaining that suffering is an expected part of it. Re-read the passage and make a list of God's gifts and promises to us (you should find at least six or seven). Why have we been given these good things (2)? What is the purpose of present sufferings? What will be our future possession? Notice that the joy of the Christian is independent of circum-stances—even in spite of suffering. Why do we rejoice?

Father, we too want to thank you for all you have done for us, all you are doing in us now and all you will do for us at the end of time. Thank you that because we belong to Jesus we are joint heirs with him. Thank you that right now you are guarding that salvation for us and us for it, so that we may receive it through faith. Amen.

Paul describes the humility of Jesus
Philippians 2 : 1–11

In our culture humility is not popular; nor has it ever been, because it may mean being less well thought of than one deserves. Jesus is the greatest example of humility because he gave up the most. What rights or position did Jesus willingly set aside? Notice the depth to which Jesus went—all without disobedience to the Father. What was the Father's response?

In context, the passage is a directive—a command for us. What does humility mean in practice (2, 3, 4)? Look up 1 Peter 5:6. What is the promise? What is the condition?

Paul puts Jesus in his place Colossians 1 : 15–23

Colossians is a letter to some Christians who faced the problem of infiltration by people called gnostics. Among their erroneous teachings was the idea that Jesus was a demi-god, simply one rung of a long ladder to God, less even than an effective mediator. In these verses Paul lifts up Jesus to his rightful place of pre-eminence as Lord of all creation and of the church. What is Jesus' relationship to the universe? It is very important to recognize that 'first-born' implies Jesus' position as Lord over the universe rather than that he is the first member of it. Notice how verse 17 clarifies this fact (*cf.* Psalm 89:27). How is Jesus related to God? For what purpose did Jesus come to earth?

Notice that Jesus became man not just to correct some wrongs (21) but also to create goodness in us (22). What is our responsibility now?

John writes about Jesus   John 3:16–21

Many years after the resurrection of Jesus, John, one of the Lord's closest friends, wrote these words about his Master's mission. What was God's motive for giving up his unique Son? (Romans 5:8 emphasizes this truth.) What other gifts, mentioned in this passage, are available to those who believe? What did Jesus *not* come to do? Why then are some people condemned? Whose fault is it? How should someone who claims to love goodness or to be a moral person respond to Jesus?

The fact is that under the searching light of Jesus' holiness all of us have things to hide. Symbolically it is the blood of Jesus which hides our sins from the holy presence of God. Our task is simply to believe that truth, accept his pardon and receive eternal life.

John writes about following Jesus 1 John 1:1—2:6

In the previous passage, John was writing to outsiders. Here he writes to believers to assure us of what we have in Jesus and also to help us recognize those who are making false claims about knowing God. Where does John get this message? Since God himself is 'light' (holiness, purity, truth), what conclusions does John draw about those who walk in darkness (who are unholy, impure, liars)? What does God promise those who walk in the light? Now compare John's analyses of those who admit no sin and those who agree with God that they do sin. God's purpose is that we should not sin (2:1, 5, 6) but he realized that, even walking in the light, we shall stumble and fall. When that happens we have someone to plead our case before God—someone who has already paid the penalty for us (2:1–2).

All of us will stumble, but the question is: Are we walking in the light, obeying God's word, walking the same way Jesus walked?

Jesus talks about the cross   Mark 10 : 35–45

James and John, the 'sons of thunder', sheepishly asked a favour of Jesus. They wanted the positions of greatest glory. The 'cup' and the 'baptism' were both pictures Jesus used when speaking of his death. What does he imply about the way to glory in God's kingdom? Romans 8:17, 18 may give you another clue. How is this different from the way things are in the kingdoms of this world (42–44)? How did Jesus demonstrate that he is the greatest servant?

In verse 45 'ransom' is used to help explain what happened on the cross. The point is not who got paid but rather that Jesus himself provided the payment. If he gave his life so that you might have new life, what value do you now have in God's eyes? Thank him.

Jesus says more about the cross   John 12 : 20–36

Jesus has just entered Jerusalem for the last time. In these words we hear the inner struggle which was part of facing the reality and ultimate purpose of his death on the cross. What would that death mean for Jesus (23)? What does it mean for us who serve him (24)? What happened to Satan (31)? What was the purpose for the rest of humanity (24, 32, 36)? Jesus said that his death meant the judgment of the world. Who, then, took the penalty which the world deserved?

Jesus loved the Father enough to glorify him even though it meant giving up his own life. What promises are ours if we follow in his steps (24–26)?

Matthew describes the cross   Matthew 27 : 27–54

The crucifixion of Jesus could hardly have been more horrible. Re-read the passage to notice how the different people showed their cruel disrespect for him. The Roman soldiers, the executioners, those who nailed the superscription to his cross, the robbers, the priests, scribes and elders all expressed contempt. What indications were there, even

28

before the resurrection, that God would have the last word?

The curtain of the temple (51) separated the court of Israel, where Jewish men could go, from the most sacred inner court of the temple, where only the high priest could enter, and he only once a year. By his death Jesus gave free access to God to all who agree with the centurion's verdict (54) and put their trust in Jesus.

John remembers the cross   John 19 : 17–30

John's account of the death of Jesus reminds us that the Gospel records are not identical but complementary. They do not disagree, but supplement each other. John tells us that Jesus was concerned about someone else—his mother—even in his own blackest hour. It is quite likely that the words of Psalm 22 were running through the Saviour's mind as he hung there in agony until thought gave way to unconsciousness and unconsciousness to death. His words 'It is finished' correspond to one Greek word meaning 'paid in full'. Jesus paid the price of all the sin of all the world for all time.

Once again, slowly think through what happened and the love which motivated the sacrifice. Allow the Holy Spirit, who inspired John's words, to give you some suitable words of thanks to God the Father.

Luke recounts the resurrection

Luke 23 : 50—24 : 12, 24

No-one could read the four Gospel accounts of the resurrection of Jesus and conclude that the writers had got together to make up the story. The records are sufficiently different in detail to make us work hard to see how they can be harmonized. But they do tell the same story, that Jesus who really died has come back to life. Put yourself in the women's place. What did they see? What did they not see? What did they hear? What did they remember? Is there any evidence that these women jumped to the conclusion that Jesus had been raised? Were the apostles predisposed to believe what the women reported to them? Did the apostles take their word for it (24)?

Not even the enemies of Jesus have ever denied that the

tomb was empty. How could you use this passage to help convince a sceptic that Jesus really rose?

Paul writes about the resurrection
1 Corinthians 15 : 1–20

This letter is our earliest written testimony to the resurrection of Jesus. Paul writes as someone who has seen the risen Lord. Who else saw him? Don't miss the importance of verse 6. Paul is inviting doubters to talk to hundreds of living eyewitnesses. The passage shows the centrality of the resurrection by listing what would *not* be true if Christ had *not* been raised. Make your own list of the logical consequences of rejecting the possibility of a resurrection.

Three times (2, 14, 17) the apostle Paul speaks of empty (vain, futile) faith. Faith which is not based on fact is worthless. If Jesus did not rise from the grave, we are of all people the most pitiful.

Father, thank you for the assurance that we have not believed in vain, and that because Jesus lives we too live and shall be raised from death at the end of time.

Jesus talks about finding new life
Luke 15 : 11–24

The key to understanding a parable is to discover the single main point which the speaker is trying to emphasize. The two preceding stories (3–10) are designed to teach the same lesson as this one. What is it? The earthly father reflects the character of our heavenly Father. What do you learn about God's attitude towards sinners? The younger son came to himself when he admitted his own need and the father's ability to meet that need.

Think or write down how you could use this passage to share the good news with someone else. Include the fact of sin, the need for repentance (turning from sin toward God), and God's willingness to forgive.

Jesus talks about starting the new life
John 3 : 1–15

Unlike many of his fellow Pharisees, Nicodemus was willing to admit that Jesus came from God, but this interview makes it clear that even that belief was not enough to make him part of God's kingdom. What else is necessary? Who accomplishes the new birth? Jesus uses one Greek word which means both wind and Spirit (8). What is he communicating through this pun? God takes the initiative, but we must respond. Verse 15 describes our part and God's promise.

Verse 14 speaks of the object of our faith without explaining it. Read John 8:28 and John 12:32 in context to see what Jesus meant by 'being lifted up'.

John talks about finding new life   John 20:24–31

How does Jesus respond to honest doubt? This passage tells us. The very fact that the Lord willingly gave signs tells us that faith is not a blind leap in the dark but trust in a person who gives real evidence of being trustworthy. What could one infer about Jesus from what is said and done on this occasion? Does Jesus accept the adoration and description which Thomas gives him?

Many people claim that they would believe *if only* Jesus would appear to them. Which verses indicate that this is not what one should expect? What has God given to us to help us 'see' Jesus and believe in him?

Paul writes about finding new life

Ephesians 2:1–10

This is one of the clearest explanations of salvation in the New Testament. A helpful way to analyse it is to think chronologically and ask yourself what actions or states are described as being in the past, the present and the future. Notice first the many descriptions of the sinner, then of the person who has been saved. Finally, see if any future action is commanded or implied. When Paul describes us as 'dead' he cannot mean completely inactive because we 'walk' and 'follow' and even 'lived in the passions of our flesh'. What does he mean? How did God change that state? What, according to verses 8 and 9, was our part in being saved?

One thing is clear: faith is not a good work by which we merit salvation, but that does not mean that good works are unnecessary. In fact, good works are part of God's eternal

31

plan for believers (10), but verse 7 reveals God's ultimate purpose.

Jesus talks about living the new life

John 15 : 1–11

Because we are saved by faith when we receive God's gift, some people get the wrong idea that we relate only to the *crucified* Christ—the sin-bearer. Not so. This passage, which applies to believers (3) describes our relationship to the *living* Christ. Repetition often points to an important theme. What word is Jesus emphasizing here? How do we abide (live) in Jesus? How do we make certain that he is abiding in us? (See verse 7 for a partial answer.) This passage is full of promises. Look for them and be sure to ask if there is any condition on which the promise rests. Notice that not all biblical promises are positive (4, 6).

The obvious purpose for keeping a vine is so that the owner can have its fruit. What does verse 8 suggest about *spiritual* fruit-bearing? What is its ultimate purpose?

Jesus explains the cost of the new life

Luke 14 : 25–33

When he died on the cross, Jesus paid the penalty for our sin. But that does not mean that being a disciple of Jesus costs us nothing. The cost is not what we offer to God (nothing) but what we must leave behind. What keeps people from being true disciples of Jesus (26, 27, 33)? Love of others is so central to the message of Jesus that verse 26 could not be teaching us to hate family and life. What does it mean? (Think about the fact that our families are usually the most important people in our lives.) As you think about verse 27, remember where Jesus was going as he carried his cross. What does this command mean in practice? Luke 9:23–25 expands this statement and might shed some light on it.

Jesus teaches about usefulness   Mark 4 : 1–20

Scripture is the best interpreter of Scripture, but the explanation is seldom as easy to find as in this passage where Jesus' own interpretation immediately follows the parable. Of the four types of people, each of whom heard the word, only one proved productive. What kept the others from displaying God's character and from reproducing themselves?

Every real Christian wants to produce the fruit his Master longs to see. Take a few minutes to examine yourself. Has God's Word sent roots deeply into your being? Are you supporting any weeds such as 'delight in riches', 'worldly cares' or 'desire for other things'? Ask God to help you seek only him.

Jesus teaches about prayer   Luke 11 : 1–13
To want to talk with God is for the Christian just as natural as a small child wanting to speak to his father. Yet, like the disciples, we may not know how. Jesus gave this prayer as an example, not as a rigid form, as you can see by comparing Matthew's version in Matthew 6:9–13. Notice the starting-point. God is given his rightful place of honour. The requirements are specific and not too wordy. One verse in the next paragraph (5–13) summarizes the teaching of the whole. Think about what it would mean if you took those words seriously. Verses 11–13 form a 'how much more' argument. What is the promise they teach?

For most of us, the problem we have with prayer is not ignorance but inertia. We spend too little time actually praying. Try praying aloud, writing prayers, praying with someone else, or using other biblical prayers to get you started.

Jesus promises his Spirit   John 14 : 15–31
This passage is packed with insights about love—Jesus' love for us and our love for him. How does Jesus show his love for the disciples he is soon to leave (and for us)? The Holy Spirit is simply the Spirit of Jesus himself, and his presence means that we are not left as *orphans* (translated 'desolate' in verse 18). What else can you learn about him from this passage? How do we show our love for Jesus? What is promised to those who love Jesus? How does Jesus show his love for the Father?

It is especially helpful to know verse 21 by heart.

Memorize both the reference (John 14:21) and the words. Don't expect to remember it without frequent revision.

Jesus promises opposition, but the Spirit's power
John 15:18-27

Verses 18–25 paint a dreary picture of the reaction of unbelievers to Jesus, the Father, and us, his followers. Why does the world have the same attitude to us as to God? The 'But' at the beginning of verse 26 implies that the situation is not hopeless. What does the Spirit do to change man's hatred of God? What were Jesus' apostles to do? How was the Spirit qualified to bear witness to Jesus? Why could the apostles testify to Jesus?

Strictly speaking, the 'you' of this passage refers to the eleven, but we are also witnesses of Christ. Since we have neither the position of the Spirit nor the privilege of being 'with Jesus from the beginning', to what may we bear witness?

Jesus describes the work of his Spirit
John 16:1-15

Jesus told his followers everything they needed to know to keep them from falling away, and then promised that his Spirit would continue to teach them the truths which would have been too much to bear at that time. Why was it to their advantage (and ours) that Christ should return to the Father? Why do unbelievers need to be convinced of the reality of sin, righteousness and judgment?

In the next verses (12–15) Jesus promises that the Spirit will give new authoritative revelation to the apostles. What is the ultimate source of this information? What does Jesus say about its character, authority and purpose? To which part of the New Testament does this seem to refer?

Jesus warns about difficult times
Mark 13:1-13

These important words of Jesus refer to 'the end times', the period between the two appearances of the Lord. Quite possibly they answer not one but three questions which puzzled the apostles (see Matthew 24:3). So although some of the events described are in the past, others are happening now and still others await fulfillment. What seem to be the greatest dangers to believers? What must happen before the end?

There is always a temptation to misapply the promises of Scripture. In what circumstances can a believer rely on the promise of verse 11? Ezra 7:10 gives one example of what Scripture commends in more normal circumstances. What is the condition connected with the promise in verse 13? To see how you can fulfill the conditions, read Jude 24, 25, and thank God.

Paul discusses the Christian life-style
Galatians 5 : 16–25

The Spirit of God gives us life, but it is not enough to be a passive recipient. What is our responsibility? How does being led by the Spirit take us from under the burden of the law (*i.e.* having to keep it all if we hope to be justified by it: 18, 23)? In your own words, describe the inner struggle which keeps us from doing what we want. How can we shift the balance of power to the side of the Spirit (see verse 24 and Romans 8:13)?

Ask God to help you recognize and turn away from those things which encourage the 'flesh'—that self-asserting, evil side of our nature—and which lead to the works of verses 19–21. Pray too that the Lord will lead you by his Spirit so that verses 22 and 23 will describe your character.

Paul describes the Christian's status
Romans 5 : 1–11

In simplest terms, to justify means to declare not guilty, or, positively, to declare righteous before the judge. No-one can *be* good enough to justify himself before God, but anyone can receive the righteousness of Christ as a free gift from Jesus who has taken our penalty (death) for us. What results of justification does Paul mention? No wonder we rejoice! What other reasons are we given for rejoicing? What is the significance of the fact that Jesus died for us while we were still sinners and enemies of God?

Meditate on the idea of hope in this passage. Where does it come from? What difference should it make in your life today?

Paul describes the Christian's freedom
Galatians 3:23—4:7

In this book Paul is explaining how those who were once slaves have been not only set free but also adopted as sons. His worry is that the sons might foolishly return to slavery. To what were the Jews enslaved? Note carefully that Paul, when read in context, is *not* against the law as a standard of life (see 5:14, 23) but only as a way of gaining acceptance before God (see 3:11; 5:3–6). How does the law bring a person to faith in Christ? What are the privileges of being God's son?

What distinctions are removed by being in Christ? Think about the implications of this radical statement of social equality.

Paul prays for his friends   Philippians 1:3–11

We all pray for those we really love. Paul is here encouraging the Philippians by telling them about his prayers for them. For what, specifically, was Paul thankful? What confidence did his observations give him (6)? What did Paul ask God to give the Philippians (9–11)? Notice the words which qualify and describe Christian love. What is the final hope which motivates us now? What will be the ultimate outcome when that is accomplished?

Notice that involvement (sharing, participation) in the gospel includes suffering (see verses 29 and 30) and thinking (27). Has being a partner in the gospel cost you anything? Thank God for the privilege (Acts 5:41).

Paul describes the Christian's armour
Ephesians 6:10–20

The committed Christian is in a battle, for he is in the advance platoon of the liberation army attacking the strongholds of this present age of darkness. Because the battle is not physical but spiritual and moral, only God's weapons and armour will protect us and have an effect against our enemy. Notice that *truth* is basic to all else. Then what else are we to add? How are we to use the sword of the Spirit? How did Jesus use it to defeat Satan (see Matthew 4:1–11)? These words of Paul contain a great

36

promise: we can stand against the Evil One. What is the condition upon which the promise rests?

Now use verses 18–20 as a guide to pray for some other Christian, especially one who is committed to sharing the truth about Jesus.

Paul rejoices in the certainty of victory
Romans 8 : 28–39

Do you ever feel that maybe even God is against you? These words should for ever dispose of any such fears. Verse 29 states God's ultimate purpose for us, and verse 30 explains how it is to take place. Follow the logic of Paul's unanswerable questions in verses 31–35. Could the God who has consistently worked for our good now abandon, condemn or deprive us? But what about circumstances (35–39)? Try to think of some circumstances which could separate you from the love of Jesus, then hold them up to the light of this passage. The reason that no circumstances can defeat us is that God is greater than circumstances and uses them for his own ends. We may *allow* ourselves to be temporarily defeated but we *need not* when we are led by the Spirit.

This passage begs to be memorized. Learn verses 28 and 32 if you are not ambitious enough to tackle the whole.

Peter's view of the new life   1 Peter 2 : 1–8

Peter stacks one metaphor on top of another in order to communicate who Jesus is in relation to the new believer. How are we to be like newborn babes? 1 Corinthians 14:20 is a passage which balances this one. What is the 'pure spiritual milk'? The imagery of the stone emphasizes that different people have differing attitudes towards Christ, and he has corresponding effects on them. What are the attitudes towards Jesus of believers? unbelievers? God? Notice that there is no place of neutrality.

Now look for the imperative verbs (those which command). Verse 4 tells us to come to Christ even though we have already come to faith in him. We need to come and feed on him daily if we are to grow up into salvation.

John's view of the new life   1 John 4 : 7–21

John's first letter was written to give believers confidence that they were God's children and to expose a certain group of heretics who were not part of God's family. One of the tests of true discipleship is love. What is our standard of love (9, 10)? Each of the three persons of the Godhead has a particular role in enabling us to love. See if you can discover them.

The fact that love can be commanded (21) is a clue that biblical love is not so much an emotion or feeling as an action—doing the loving thing—sacrificing one's self for the good of someone else. Loving God may seem easy until we realize that it means obeying him and loving both our brothers and sisters and our enemies. This would be impossible had not God taken up residence within us. Because he has, and because we live in him, we are able to love with his love in this world.

David sings to God our shepherd   Psalm 23

These familiar and comforting words were written by a man who knew God's will and wrote honestly about what the relationship meant to him. They tell us much about God, the Good Shepherd. Any metaphor requires that we first think about the earthly picture which is being used to communicate eternal truth. What does a shepherd provide for his sheep? What does God give us? Where does God lead us? What is our comfort even in difficult circumstances? In verse 5 the metaphor changes to a banquet scene. Notice that nothing is lacking.

Meditate on verse 1. With God as our protector and provider we will not be without any good thing. Thanks be to God!

David sings about truth   Psalm 19

God reveals himself to us through creation and through his written Word, which in turn reveals to us the living Word, Jesus. This psalm has something to say about the first two means of revelation. What can we learn about God from his creation (1–6)? Romans 1:19–20 may give you a clue. But creation marred by man's rebellion says little about God's moral nature. How does the psalmist describe God's Scriptures (spoken of here as law, testimony, precepts, commandment, ordinances)? What should our attitude be towards the Bible? What specifically can the Bible do for us?

The Bible often shows us our shortcomings, warns us of the dangers of sin and explains the way of deliverance from slavery to sin. Meditate on verses 12–14 until you can make this your own prayer and offer it to God from the heart.

David sings about strength   Psalm 18 : 1–19

When Saul rejected God, God rejected him as king of Israel and allowed an evil spirit to dominate his life. That spirit drove him to try to murder David. David wrote this poetic song when he was delivered from one of Saul's attacks. As in all poetry the language is figurative, so David is not saying that God is literally a rock or that he has nostrils or ears or feet. What is he saying? See if you can find one verse which summarizes the whole message of the psalm.

It is important to notice that God was David's refuge *before* trouble arose. What did David do *when* he was under attack? What did God do?

Verse 19 (and indeed the rest of the psalm) reminds us that God does not deliver everyone, but only those who take a righteous stand against God's enemies. Examine yourself. Is God your refuge? Are you his representative?

David sings about forgiveness   Psalm 32

Some of David's psalms may leave an impression of self-righteousness. In fact, David is not protesting his own innocence, but asking God to deliver him as one who is righteous by association with God's name and cause. In Psalm 32, a teaching psalm (maskil), David makes it plain that he sins like everyone else. What happened to David when he tried to hide his sin? What happened when David admitted his sin to God? Look for all the phrases which describe David's new condition.

Some people think that confession and forgiveness are simply techniques in personal relationships. In fact, they are God's means of reconciling us to himself. They work because he is real and his Word is true.

Memorize Proverbs 28:13.

The different styles of literature in the Bible

Part of the uniqueness of the Bible lies in the fact that it is both a book and a library. The remarkable unity of the whole is blended from varied ingredients written over at least a millennium, by around forty authors with countless assistants, and in a variety of styles. We need to appreciate these styles if we are to hear the whole message.

The Jews traditionally divide the Old Testament into the Law, the Prophets and the Writings. The Law (Genesis to Deuteronomy) begins with poetic accounts of the origins of man and his problems, merging into traceable history which includes the statistics and rule of life of the Jews under Moses. The Prophets includes history books (Samuel, Kings, *etc.*) as well as the distilled message of later spokesmen for God such as Isaiah and Malachi, whose words need to be understood in their historical context. The Writings contain many things— the hymnbook of Psalms, a love song and a love story, the reflections of Ecclesiastes and Job, and a great collection of ancient sayings connected by reference to God and called Proverbs.

The New Testament is set apart from the Old by 400 years and by the intervention of Jesus. Its earliest parts are the Epistles, ranging from personal letters like Philemon and 2 John, through businesslike pastoral messages and sermonettes, to treatises of the weight of Romans and Hebrews. The Gospels are in a class of their own, stories of a man's life which, though not fiction, are more than just biography. Revelation, like Daniel, is an apocalyptic piece, in which a visionary is given by God an insight into other-worldly reality which is relevant to the here-and-now.

In practice, we must be careful to read and interpret the different parts as what they are, not expecting them to be what they are not. Poetry, history and sermon can all teach doctrine, but they will do it in different ways. If we miss this we will interpret wrongly (see p. 24) and apply it mistakenly.

2. The Jesus story

At a certain stage in the early days of Christianity, the need arose to write gospels. Many people, who had not been in contact with Jesus in his lifetime, were becoming Christians, and many more were expressing interest. It became necessary to write the story of Jesus, so that enquirers could examine the evidence, and so that Christians could live by his teaching and pass on his message. Many people in our own day have a similar need for facts; the following studies set out to explore them.

A Prince of Peace   Isaiah 9 : 1–7
Jesus was born to a forward-looking race, who had long anticipated the birth of a princely child from God. None of their leaders, priests or kings, had ever measured up to the picture they longed to see. God, they were sure, would send an heir of David to bring wisdom, strength and justice to the leadership of his people in their land. Out of Galilee would come a figure bringing light for gloom, joy for pressure, peace for tension; he would inaugurate an indestructible era and kingdom, undergirded by God. Under Rome, some had given up hoping . . .

A son is given   Luke 2 : 1–21
It happens every few seconds across the world today. That night, plotted in history by Luke's pinpoint accuracy, it happened to an unmarried mum in a grubby outhouse. The birth was ordinary, but what did Mary make of its significance in her pondering (19)—especially in the light of her experience in chapter 1:26–56? In one short passage the new child is designated as Saviour, Christ, Lord and Jesus—all titles worth meditating on. Letting the local shepherds into the secret was God's signal that this child, and the news about him, was for the most ordinary of people.
　　Memorize Isaiah 9:6.

Prepare the way   Luke 3 : 1–14

Jesus' older cousin John seems to have been using the
desert quiet to pray and listen for God; now he bursts on the
Judaean scene. As a prophet, the first since Old Testament
days, he proclaims water baptism to signify forgiveness and
the washing from old ways and entrance into a new life. As
the long-expected herald of God's coming, he fulfils a word
to Isaiah. He assails the false confidence of the Jews who
believed in an automatic salvation on the grounds of their
nationality. As a teacher, he takes authority to show all comers (including Roman soldiers) the style of life appropriate to
God's coming.

Then Jesus came   Matthew 3 : 11–17

John makes incredible claims for Jesus. He will outstrip
John, offering a new life as much richer than John's as the
Spirit of God is richer than the river Jordan. He has the right
to sift people apart, keeping his own and destroying the rest.
He has no need to repent in John's baptism. John's God also
testifies; for when Jesus does stand along with the others in
baptism, the Spirit marks him out, and the voice from
heaven hints at kingship (Psalm 2:7) and divine service
(Isaiah 42:1).

Led by the Spirit   Matthew 4 : 1–11

It is notable that for Jesus, a new phase of service for God
was not marked by escape from opposition or evil; the Spirit
of God pushed him straight into confrontation. There is no
suggestion, here or elsewhere in the New Testament, that
Jesus or his followers viewed the devil as a shorthand term
for impersonal evil in general; he was real, personal and
dangerous. Here he entices Jesus to abuse his powers, his
status and his mission. Jesus resists him by reference to
Scripture (Deuteronomy 8:3; 6:16; 6:13), in one case in the
face of Satan's own abuse of Scripture.

*Lord, help me to face temptation and conquer it in the strength
of your Spirit.*

The magnet starts working   John 1 : 35–51

Andrew and (probably) Philip are the first of a long and growing line of people drawn by this remarkable man. They make three significant transitions: of interest, from John to Jesus; of understanding, from the teacher to the Christ; and of action, from sitting and listening to sharing the news and inviting others. The immediate effect is to enlarge the Jesus group. Simon is recruited and his future redirected; sceptical Nathanael is won over and offered more than even he now understands. Seven more titles for Jesus here: why not start listing them and exploring their meaning?

Jesus goes public   Mark 1 : 14–28

John had warned that God's time was near; Jesus claimed that it had arrived. More apparently arrogant still, he said that God's coming was tied up with his own (see Luke 4:16–21). He now mobilizes the kingdom's agent, and proclaims its message in strategic Capernaum. (Several trade and communication routes passed through Galilee, and Capernaum helped service them.) In Jesus, authority in teaching truth was combined with authority over spirit forces, indicating the presence of a powerful worker for God. His kingdom would quickly draw widespread attention—and just as rapidly, opposition.

Public and private   Mark 1 : 29–45

'Moved with pity' (41) is a characteristic term for Jesus, meaning (precisely) 'having a gut-reaction of concern'. This compassion is a mark of his ministry, extending to every kind of need; hunger, bondage, sickness, loss of purpose or direction. The range of his concern, and his power to act upon it, give his work the makings of a mass movement. Behind it all we are shown his private priorities; prayer to renew his power, and a longing to proclaim God's message. The need for truth runs even deeper than the need to relieve suffering.

Lord, help us to see you more clearly.

Signs of the times   John 2 : 1–11

John uses the story to highlight the whole way Jesus worked. His compassion even went to work to stop embarrassment spoiling a couple's big day. When he acted, there was not only power but a signpost, pointing to something. Jesus could take something ordinary—a human life, a marriage, Jewish ways—and turn it into something special. The Jews were in danger if they only looked back to their law; for God had kept the best until now.

Is it fair to treat verse 5 as 'the gospel according to Mary'?

The skin bursts   Mark 2 : 13–22

Jesus criticized the Jewish religious leaders for treating God's truth as their private property, and sitting on it so that others would not enjoy it (see Matthew 25 : 14–30). He went in for popular religion. Unlike the bookworms, he could draw a crowd and make them listen. He would shock the prudish Pharisees by mixing with all comers, and if they needed forgiveness, good—he had come to bring it. And he put their pious habits in the shade by stressing the drastic newness of his own ways. What claim is implied by calling himself the bridegroom here?

Memorize verse 17.

Sound and fury   Luke 6 : 1–11

Even today a Jew can be criticized for taking a child to the Wailing Wall on Friday afternoon, when the sabbath is starting; 'How can he push the pram home without breaking the law?' The Pharisees were right to stress the law, but wrong in their rigid, hair-splitting application. Jesus reproached them for their unbalanced reading of Scripture, their loveless attitude to need, and their negative approach to goodness. But he also coolly provoked their anger by showing them up in public, disagreeing with them over the sabbath, and comparing himself with King David.

44

Night of the long future Luke 6 : 12–26

Jesus prayed in depth over these key men who were to
graduate from disciple to apostle, from learner to
messenger. It was typical of him to encourage them with a
new display of his power; his resources would be theirs.
Typical, too, to warn of the pressures they would face. The
'beatitudes' show up how radically Christ would turn things
upside down; but in the process disciples and apostles
together would have to face resentment along with their
blessing. His call to service promises power, hope and joy;
but not without cost.

I am the life Luke 7 : 11–23

A great crowd went with him, the report spread, he cured
many . . . but here as so often he stops everything for an individual. You can see Nain from Nazareth: perhaps he knew
the woman. His potent compassion gives life to the lonely,
broken mother as much as to the son. His own commentary
on this power of his can be read in John 11. (Who else did
Jesus raise from death?) While many Christians apologize for
Jesus' miracles, he would boldly use them as evidence. Here
he does so for his depressed cousin John, giving him life too.

Two storms calmed Mark 4 : 35—5 : 15

There had always been difficulty fitting Jesus into a tidy
category; carpenter, prophet, sorcerer . . . Now the question
becomes urgent: 'Who is this?' One group of shaken people
sees the lake whipped by the winds funnelling down through
the hills; then they watch Jesus calmly take the prerogative
of God to handle nature. Another group sees the lake
foaming with dead pigs, and finds this same man talking
calmly to the local madman. Both groups are awestruck.
There are only two possible reactions—to close the mind
(5:17) or to open it wide enough to take him in.

Please, Lord, deepen our confidence in you.

45

Not drinking water   John 4 : 1–15
It was not done for a man to approach a woman in public, still less a moral outcast (hence her midday visit alone; see too verses 16–26). Nor could a Jew approach a Samaritan across their historic racio-political divide. Jesus crashes these barriers to meet her at depth, gently shifting her attention from her prejudices to himself, from her thirst to his offer, from her earthbound thinking to his promise of heaven-sent refreshment. But, as the sequel shows, he has to pierce her conscience before he can meet her need.

Memorize verse 14.

Two debtors   Luke 7 : 36–50
In Jesus' world, the attention and the implied dignity he gave to women were quite revolutionary. Strikingly, two that we have looked at (and others he met) were broken women; yet he could get close enough to restore them without his motives being suspect. A rare man! He does not suggest that her love earns her forgiveness; the debtor story reverses the logic and says forgiveness leads to love. Our indebtedness to Christ is measured by our warmth towards him and others; hence the criticism of Simon, also (pointedly) a debtor, for snootily withholding the basic courtesies.

Treasure still hidden   Matthew 13 : 44–58
Jesus highlights the curious mixture of attitudes people adopt towards the kingdom of God which he has inaugurated. Some find it rich and precious, rejoicing when they stumble upon it or hunting until they find it. Others masquerade as members of it and will not be sorted out until he tests their genuineness himself at the end of time. Others again, especially where familiarity has bred contempt, brush it aside and prevent Christ being effective near them. How do you honestly answer the question in verse 54? (We return to the kingdom theme below, pp. 167 ff.)

Coming and going   Mark 6 : 30–44

Look at Jesus' attitude to planning! His inner circle have had
a trial mission by themselves (7–13), and Jesus wants a rest
(notably) for them and a chance to reflect together on the
lessons learnt. When a crowd of people get in the way, they
don't spoil it at all, and he is not frustrated. His compassion
is stirred by their need—not physical need this time, but
sheer human lostness. The answer is not a meal but several
hours' teaching; only then does his love turn to their
stomachs. And the disciples didn't miss their seminar after
all. Contrast the end of verse 31 with verse 42; what does it
say about Christian work?

Lord, help us to share your compassion and act on it.

Sink or stand   Matthew 14 : 22–33

For many, the experience of Peter is an illustration of
Christian living. Daringly accepting an invitation from Christ,
he found himself doing the impossible; shifting his focus
from Christ to the circumstances around himself, he began
to slip; calling wisely for help, he received it and was
rescued; and others noticed.

Is this figurative use of the Bible correct? If not, what can
the story say to us now? If so, how might you apply it to
yourself?

On the side of God   Mark 8 : 27–38

After watching Jesus preside at the feeding of the five
thousand, the disciples are at a turning-point in their understanding of him. Beyond popular misconception they can
see that he is God's commissioned envoy; only now can
Jesus take them further and explain that part of his role will
be to suffer. This, and the cost of going with him, is too
much as yet; but they are beginning to see how big the decision is—to do with gaining or losing a life. And somehow
that decision will be underwritten in the future by the same
Jesus.

Good to be here
Mark 9 : 2–13

The Caesarea Philippi turning-point is climaxed by this vision for the 'inner circle' of Peter, James and John. Why did Jesus meet Moses and Elijah and not, for example, Abraham, David or Daniel? What do we learn from Peter's impulse to turn the moment into an institution?

There was much current talk about Elijah's expected return to precede God's coming (see Malachi 4:5, 6, Mark 8:28). Jesus pins this role onto John the Baptist, now dead (Mark 6:14–29), adding that they ought to study the Scriptures equally closely in order to understand him, the Son of man.

Not able
Mark 9 : 14–29

Jesus contrasts with his disciples at several points. They wanted to build huts on the mountain to enjoy God; he went back to meet human need. They could not deal with this longstanding problem; he could. They stood about bickering with the scribes; he acted. They had no comfort for the boy's father; Jesus drew the father's faith forward as well as helping his son. The disciples were baffled by their failure; Jesus knew the source of power well enough to direct them to it. All these point us to pray the prayer of verse 24 for ourselves.

Rules of membership (i)
Mark 9 : 30–48

This little cluster of incidents and comments throws light on what is involved in going with Jesus. We need to weigh the aspect of suffering in his work, and its continuing effect on us (30–32). We have to learn that greatness with him lies in service and humility, not wealth and power (33–37). We need to be careful of pulling his boundaries too tight, and shutting out some who really belong (38–41). We have to strengthen the simple, not undermine their faith (42). And we need to be ready to sacrifice things which impede our flat-out involvement with him (43–48).

Find a suitable verse to memorize from this passage.

Rules of membership (ii)   Luke 9:57—10:12

The first man seems to have been jumping on the bandwagon, the second shilly-shallying, and the third going back on his word. Jesus warns all three that commitment to him is tough, serious and once-for-all.

The seventy's orders are not universal, though many Christians are called to work like this for a time. The principles do stand for all: there is plenty to do, and Christ's people must travel light to do it. Our lives should speak of God, and the reception we get will reflect how he is received.

Rules of membership (iii)   Luke 10:25-41

It is one thing to live Christian standards to a minimum, avoiding blatant wrongdoing; it is quite another to keep their spirit positively. Jesus urges a love which takes risks, includes unlikely people, is generous with our own resources and accepts sacrifice. The Samaritan's two pence suggests planned and long-term caring which refuses to pass the buck. This is not a recipe for Martha's frantic and busy do-gooding, but for quietly loving service which finds room to listen to the Lord's voice.

Lord, help me to love all my neighbours.

Stopping the scattering   Luke 11:14-28

The attempt to assess Jesus—and to discredit him—continues. Now they try to brand him with being in league with the devil. He demolishes their logic and turns their own argument upon them—then rams home his own. If he controls evil without sharing it, then his power must be God's, and those who reject him are frustrating God. The claim was large and the challenge sharp. Can you think of current false views of Christ which must be resisted if this work is not to be frustrated? How do verses 24-26 apply to the Christian today?

Practical application

The Bible constantly emphasizes that we should not only *hear* God's Word, but *do* it. It is not always easy, however, to see *how* to apply what it says.

The first step is to understand what the Bible is really saying. We need to know the meaning of its words and the context in which they are used. We must allow for the different styles of literature in the Bible (see p. 40), and the specific situations in which, or to which, different parts were written; specific instructions may be universal in application, or local and temporary—'Go not to Egypt' hardly still applies! But the *principle* does (in this case, the principle of trusting God rather than a strong but godless human power). As for the narrative parts, God may give us these for straight information, as examples, or as warnings; the example of Judas is different from that of Paul.

Secondly, we should be alive to all the areas of life to which Scripture will apply. The Bible will not only change our moral behaviour, but our spiritual life, doctrinal beliefs, and personal relationships. It will go beyond us as individuals and speak to our families and local fellowships to the church of Christ at large and to the whole society in which it is set. As we read, our ears have to be open for guidance at all these levels. 'You shall not steal' is universal, but its consequences in practice will differ for different groups.

Thirdly, in practice, application is largely a matter of setting our own life alongside the meaning of the Bible as a yardstick. We can see our praying beside Christ's, our penitence beside David's in Psalm 51, or our love beside 1 Corinthians 13. Where there are discrepancies we can begin to pray and ask the Lord by his Spirit to add and subtract as necessary; then we shall begin to cultivate what God commends and cut out what he hates. See Romans 6; Galatians 5:16–26; Colossians 3 and Acts 15 for guidance about making the real changes needed, individually and in the life together of Christ's people. Remember that some changes can be almost immediate, while others will need a process of thought, prayer and discipline over months.

Giving him a hearing John 7 : 37–52

The feast of tabernacles included the pouring of water daily in the temple, as a sign of God's goodness and a prayer for next season's rain. In this highly charged situation Jesus intervened at the climax of the week, claiming to offer by his Spirit a deeper and better refreshment than either physical water or Judaism could. People again divided as they tried to fit Jesus into their mental categories and their understanding of Scripture. Despite the Pharisees' anger, the guard would not seize him; despite their contempt, Nicodemus (see John 3) found the courage to stand up to them.

RSVP Luke 14 : 15–24

Jesus' blunt words at supper about generosity are piously taken up by another guest, and Jesus is equally blunt about the banquet of the kingdom. Many with the privilege in their background or education of knowing about the kingdom are patronizingly turning it down. Familiarity, now as then, breeds contempt. In consequence God has flung it wide open and the most unlikely can come in: un-Jewish, untaught, uncouth, un-rich—these are the people Jesus came for. Would you agree that people characteristically use property, business and home as excuses?

I shall not want John 10 : 1–18

Jesus was fond of the shepherd-and-sheep image (see Luke 15:1–7). Here he draws all its Old Testament significance (Psalm 23, Jeremiah 23:1–6, Ezekiel 34) down upon himself. Don't be confused by the 'door of the sheep' (7–9); it speaks of the way the shepherd himself lay across the sheepfold entrance, watching their comings and goings and guarding against intruders. So it emphasized a further aspect of the shepherd role. To get beyond the pretty picture, list real ways in which the passage has meaning for you. Hunt out Jesus' other 'I am' claims in John.

Learn verses 10 and 11.

Your King is coming　　　　　　　　Mark 11 : 1–11

The climax of Jesus' life comes after a steady, deliberate
march on Jerusalem, arriving as the city was swollen with
visitors for the Passover. Coming up the long climb from
Jericho to Bethany, behind the Mount of Olives (have a look
at a map), he stage-manages a visual aid for the crowd.
Matthew points to the propehcy in Zechariah 9:9 which
Jesus was consciously fulfilling. Coming in peace, he
nevertheless put on a demonstration of popular support
which alarmed the authorities and renewed speculation
about his identity and intentions (Matthew 21:10).

Lord, I praise you for your kingship and your courage.

Looking for fruit　　　　　　　　Mark 11 : 12–25

The coming of the King of peace is followed by a strikingly
sharp offensive. Jesus turns furiously on the corrupt com-
mercialism of the temple, and then articulates his protest in
the very place where teachers of authority were heard. No-
one dares challenge him openly (Mark 14:49). In this context the blighting of the fig tree makes sense: it is a stark
commentary on God's attitude to the fruitlessness of
Jerusalem. The converse is the reassurance given to Peter
about prayer: God loves to give answers and resources to
those who want to bear fruit for him.

They will respect my son　　　　　　Mark 12 : 1–11

Jesus' offensive continues, with a very uncomplimentary
summary of Jewish history (see Isaiah 5:1–12 for the
background). Every messenger of God has had a hard time
at the hands of those currently in charge of the nation. (For
example, see Jeremiah 36 or Ezekiel 2 and 3.) As if this were
not enough, he implies his own superiority to the venerated
prophets and almost dares them to kill him; then he adds
that if they do God will vindicate him at their expense. Why
was he so provocative? Was he right about being vindicated—and if so, how did it happen?

Quite wrong   Mark 12 : 18–27

The Sadducees appear to have been an aristocratic group of the priesthood, stand-offish in manner and too respectable in theology, in reluctant league with the Pharisees. They stuck tightly to the first five books of the Scriptures and had no time for logical deductions from the rest, such as a future life. Disdaining enthusiasm or popular religion, their question is designed to ridicule Jesus. He shows bluntly that he understands the Scriptures, the power of God and the future much more profoundly than they. Depth can be simple, and sophistication shallow.

Words that stick   Mark 13 : 24–37

This period of Jesus' ministry is marked by no end of forward glimpses (compare John 14). Like much Old Testament prophecy, Mark 13 is concerned with a two-stage future event, immediate and ultimate. On the immediate level, the power of the kingdom erupted at Pentecost and its matching judgment fell on Jerusalem in AD 70; ultimately, we still await the glorious coming of the Son of man. While the fact is certain the timing is hidden, so that we neither panic nor take our ease meanwhile. How do you grapple with verse 30?

Learn verse 31.

Giving a hand   Mark 14 : 10–25

As the passover meal happens the film seems to slip into slow motion while Jesus moves (and is moved) so gradually on to his death. Across this huge screen, in pathetic contrast to Jesus, flits a small-minded Judas—politically frustrated, personally jealous or just after the money? Equally shadowy is the small helping hand of the man with the room. And in Jesus' hands one loaf and one cup of wine become, alongside baptism, the greatest visual aids in Christianity. What is the covenant (24)?

53

Example of love   John 13 : 1–15
John greatly enlarges our knowledge of the last supper
(chapters 13 to 17). The disciples still stand on their dignity,
none doing the slave's job of washing the travellers' feet.
Jesus sets out to reinforce one of his own lessons (Matthew
20:20–28) and makes his meaning plain (12–15). In the
process Peter gives him the opportunity, quickly taken, to
rub home another lesson (6–10). Jesus provides a new status
(cleanness) for which the new life-style (service) is appropriate. Could you link the main features of Jesus' life into
the brilliant summary in verse 1? Look too at the interaction
between Judas and Satan.

Help me to follow your example, Lord.

Study in contrasts (i)   Mark 14 : 32–50
Here Jesus, all too aware, reveals his humanity as nowhere
else; his prayer is an agony of mind and will reflected in
Christian experience ever since. The disciples' drowsiness is
more than physical, as is Jesus' call to 'watch'; the next few
hours show up their lamentable dullness to the issues about
to be settled. As for the authorities, Jesus spotlights an un-
derhandedness which stands at the heart of every knock-in-
the-night arrest which has followed. At the end only Jesus
seems in control of himself—and of events. What might his
'Watch' mean today?

Study in contrasts (ii)   Luke 22 : 54–71
Peter's collapse is a bitter reminder to any of Christ's people
who have been challenged over their allegiance and funked
it; all the worse beside the dignity and courage of Jesus
himself. Again the authorities and their strong-men are hardly distinguished by concern for humanity or sound judicial
principles (see the other Gospel accounts for more detail).
Looking at all four Gospels, what do you make of the reports
of Jesus' words? Why the apparent confusion? Was he
himself dodging the issue, or just refusing to be trapped in
their precast form of words?

Study in contrasts (iii)
Luke 23 : 1–25

Most of us flap under pressure; the quiet steadiness of Jesus holds in the face of a shabby shuffle to find someone who will take responsibility. He stands back from the politically slanted formula fed to Pilate, and from the frivolity of Herod. He copes with manhandling and mob hysteria, and significantly steps into the shoes of a real wrongdoer so that he goes free. (See the New English Bible for Matthew's artistic handling of this: Matthew 27: 11–26.) It is easy to condemn—but what alternative had Caiaphas, Pilate or Herod? Does verse 12 speak to you of a modern reality?

Our passover lamb
Exodus 12 : 1–14

It would be a mistake to rush into the story of Jesus' death without some idea of the background which gave it significance. The Jewish Paul coined the phrase 'Christ our passover (or paschal) lamb' to refer to Jesus' death (1 Corinthians 5:7). Jesus again deliberately used a Jewish festival to highlight his own role, reapplying the main features in a new way; judgment was to fall, but the death of God's lamb instead protected his people and allowed them to escape from slavery. Likewise the Lord's supper reapplies the passover meal to commemorate the new Lamb and the new exodus.

The man of sorrows
Isaiah 52 : 13—53 : 12

The figure whom Isaiah portrays in his 'Servant Songs' has some affinities with the whole Jewish nation, and some with their idea of a servant-king, but the full picture will be confined to neither. God is clearly giving the prophet a vision of an ideal figure to come, who will serve God truly and set the people free from sin by his suffering. Phrases from these songs occur at crucial moments in Jesus' life (Mark 1:11; 9:7) and in his own teaching about himself (Mark 10:45). Only Calvary can fulfil this dark but wonderful expectation.
Learn Isaiah 53:6.

The Lamb of God   Leviticus 4 : 27–35

Hebrews 8–10 is the New Testament's commentary on this passage. The seriousness of sin was underlined to the Jews by the need for a bull (3), goat or lamb to die in order to purge it: 'without the shedding of blood there is no forgiveness of sins' (Hebrews 9:22). Reconciliation with God was possible by this means, mechanical and inadequate as it was. But the whole system was but a foreshadowing and a visual aid for the true sacrifice which opened the way to God and rendered the temple system redundant. Compare verses 32–34 with Isaiah 53:4–7.

The King of the Jews   Psalm 22

Jewish ideas of God's servant were largely focused in the representative figure of the king. He ruled them for God, prayed for them, led them in war, and carried their suffering in times of hardship or defeat. This psalm was originally an expression of the king's desolation in that suffering role, and was clearly in Jesus' mind as he hung on the cross. At the same time, a sobering amount of circumstantial detail is here almost eerily foreshadowed. Can you list the parts which tie into the Gospel accounts?

The Christ of God   Luke 23 : 26–43

Even in the midst of this grim experience Jesus seems to attend more to other people than to his own suffering. He finds words of foresight and warning for the women, of forgiveness for his killers, of comfort and promise for the dying criminal beside him. By contrast Luke records no response to the mocking of verses 35 to 37. How might we answer Jesus' question (31) or respond to the rulers' challenge (35)? Take time to visualize the scene and thank him for it. Ask yourself which of the characters here you identify with most closely.

Finished John 19:23–37

John packs this terse account with implications. He underlines the faithfulness of the women followers (compare the men), Jesus' control over events (compare appearances), and the reality of his death. He refers three times to scriptures fulfilled. He gives us three more pointed phrases from Jesus: the first secures protection for his mother (incidentally shedding light on Matthew 12:46–50); the second could hardly declare his humanity more simply and movingly. The third—'Finished!'— means *completed*, and was the word used for bills that were paid. It was a cry not of failure but of triumph.

Peter reflects 1 Peter 2:20–25; 3:18–22

The next four readings bring out the significance which four New Testament writers saw in the central event of the cross. Peter, for whom the memory must have been bitter, recalls Jesus' trial along with his death. For him Jesus was (i) an example of uncomplaining submission in the face of injustice, trusting a just God to put things right; (ii) a once-for-all replacement for us, taking God's wrath so that he could give us God's life; (iii) a risen protector whose death gave him the right to govern and care for a new order.

Learn 2:24 and 3:18.

Paul reflects Romans 5:1–11

Embedded in the heart of this great exposition of the Christian faith is Paul's list of the good things which Christ's death has made available: (i) our past antagonism ('sinners', 'enemies') is reconciled: we have peace with God. (ii) Our past exclusion from God's presence ('ungodly', under 'the wrath of God') is overcome in our being made right by the rightness of Christ (justification): we have access to God again. (iii) Our past hopelessness ('helplessness') is ended by the arrival of the loving, powerful Spirit: we rejoice in our hope of sharing God's glory, and can thus face the pressures of the present.

Another reflects
Hebrews 9:6–14

Whoever wrote this message was trying to dissuade Christians from being drawn into Judaism. Here he contrasts the old sacrificial system and the great sacrifice of Christ. (i) Outer and inner: the old sacrifices happened in a visible place and dealt with ritual uncleanness; Christ's was effective in heaven and cleansed the conscience. (ii) Partial and perfect: all the temple paraphernalia managed only a limited nearness to God; Jesus' death opened the way to God's inner presence (see Mark 15:37, 38). (iii) Repeated and final: the priests had to sacrifice 'continually'; Jesus 'entered once for all' to secure a much more radical forgiveness.

John reflects
Revelation 1:4–20

Here we are presented with a vision of Christ in glory. Both the seer and the one he sees emphasize the centrality of the cross as the key to his glory and his right to speak with authority to the churches (5, 7, 18). The vision stresses (i) his humanity: the ambivalent title 'Son of man' is Jesus' own favourite for himself; *a* man who is *the* man of God; (ii) his purity: whiteness, flame, being refined are all symbols of the absence of dirt or corruption; (iii) his glory: the weakness of Calvary is transfigured into rule and kingship—as he had foretold.

I have seen the Lord
John 20:1–18

Even former sceptics now assert that John's Gospel originates with an eyewitness; and certainly this passage has a first-hand flavour. The unexpectedness of the resurrection to the disciples is brought out, undermining the argument that they fantasized it out of preconditioned minds. The reality of it is highlighted by several little touches: the stone rules out women moving it, the cloths rule out grave-robbers, the appearance to Mary rules out fiction (no Jewish man would concoct a story resting so hard on female evidence). What does the interview with Mary teach about the nature of Jesus' new life?

58

Why question?   Luke 24 : 36–49

There is more on the resurrection on p. 30. Here Jesus
himself brings some facts before the doubters: (i) He himself,
as risen, was too material to be confused with any dream,
hallucination or spirit; none of them eats fish. (ii) His own
previous teaching has pointed this way, based upon and
fulfilling the Scriptures of the Old Testament. (iii) The
worldwide mission of Christ's people, then only in prospect
but now well known, would be evidence of the reality of the
sender. (iv) The power of his Spirit among Christians would
(and did) also convince; if there were no risen Christ, there
would be no Spirit from him.

My witnesses   Acts 1 : 1–11

The disciples want to know when it will all be over; Jesus
gently steers them off speculation on to the realities he has
for them. (i) Power: the Spirit, promised and soon to come,
who would equip them for new levels of love, self-giving and
effectiveness. (ii) Work: the whole world lay before them, to
be reached in circles from Jerusalem, omitting no-one. They
were to be *witnesses*; people needed the news of Jesus, not
just its consequences. (iii) Glory: the cloud in which Jesus
withdrew marked the presence and greatness of God, in
which he will return triumphantly at the end.

The end of Jesus' earthly life is by no means the end of
his activity. Luke's second volume, which we now call the
Acts of the Apostles, gives the account of the coming of
Jesus' promised Spirit and the outburst of witness which he
brought about. We look at this story in outline from p. 106.
The story, of course, has unfolded ever since, and still goes
on; this is why we now turn to some studies on practical
Christian living for ourselves today.

3. Aspects of Christian living

Becoming a Christian, according to Paul's teaching, makes you a new person altogether (2 Corinthians 5:17). We have seen in the initial studies of this book that the heart of the gospel is Christ; it is he who transforms our lives, who makes us new people. It is possible to read the story of Jesus and to fail to give him your heart and life—such is Satan's power.

This next section is a hard look at the practical implications of following Christ. Its style is different from what has gone before in that it asks more rhetorical questions. The questions are often simple and yet they are awkward; they are the basic questions which need to be faced and answered honestly if we are to make any progress as a Christian. Many unhappy and 'stale' Christians are in such a plight because they haven't got these fundamental principles sorted out. The joy of a useful and fulfilled life is only for those who take God at his word.

Believing

Seeing
John 1 : 1–13

The beginning of the Christian life is an eye-opener. The testimony of the Christian is, 'Though I was blind, now I see.' The first stage, then, is to recognize who Jesus is. These verses describe him as author of the universe (1–4) and the light of the world (5–9). He is unrecognized and therefore rejected by many (10, 11), but those who recognize him accept him and trust him. Believing is not a leap in the dark, but a leap into the light, a liberation into seeing things the way they really are. Have you seen him yet?

Receiving
Luke 19 : 1–10

This story illustrates the experience of becoming a Christian. Zacchaeus wants to identify Jesus, but finds it difficult on account of the crowd and his own limitations (3). But he persists (4), and to his amazement his interest has not gone unnoticed by Christ, who invites himself into his home (5). The reception is joyful and speedy (6), in the face of opposition (7), and immediately results in a changed life. New people in Christ always have changed morals. Believing is receiving—no academic knowledge at a safe distance. Have you received him yet?

Acknowledging
Romans 10 : 1–13

Being a Christian is not just being sincere (2). Any confidence in our own ability to please God is misplaced (3) and the only thing that makes us fit for God's presence is Christ's sacrificial fulfilment of the law on our behalf (4). We do not have to make special journeys (6, 7) but we do have to trust God's crowning testimony to Jesus' identity (the resurrection) and publicly acknowledge our new-found allegiance (9). Believing and acknowledging cannot be divorced. Secret discipleship is out (10). Do you acknowledge him yet—both privately and publicly?

61

Living and dying

Counting the cost   Luke 14 : 25–33

The setting is a great crowd of people. Christ, whom they are following, turns to warn them about where he will lead them and what it will involve. Allegiance must be supremely to him (26), and considerations of personal safety and pleasure must go out of the window (27). A sober reckoning must be made before starting (28–31). Not every contingency can be envisaged, but the toughness of the enterprise must not be doubted. Being a Christian affects every area of your life—home, career, time, money, interests, friendships. Think about your life. Are you prepared to pay the price (33)?

Following   Luke 9 : 23–27, 57–62

Discipleship never was and never will be the easy option. Self must not be considered, but denied; life must not be saved, but lost (23, 24). Profit is to be seen in personal rather than material terms (25) and there can be no divorce of Christ's person from his words (26). Seeing the kingdom is the most important and thrilling thing in the world. Nevertheless, his way will be uncomfortable (58) and his demands absolute (59, 60). Procrastination is out, and half-hearted commitment disqualifies one from his lordship (61, 62).

Paying the cost   Philippians 1 : 19–30

Paul is writing from prison (13), a clear case of the persecutor choosing to become the persecuted (look up Acts 22:4). He does not minimize his suffering or his hope for deliverance, but testifies that both life and death have a new perspective because of Christ (21). It is tremendous when you can say that Christ dominates your horizon (23, 24), that intimacy with him matters to you—a longing to die (23); that pleasing him matters to you—a longing to serve (24). If his glory is your supreme concern (27), then there is no doubt that you will suffer for it (28, 29).

Knowing

The first witness—what God says 1 John 5 : 1–12

Assurance is ours when we fix our attention on his character and testimony (9); doubt is ours when we concentrate on the quality of our belief (3: 19, 20). Conviction of the reality of our status as children of God may come slowly. It comes by meditating on God's testimony to Jesus, which he gave in three ways: (i) by the *Spirit*, when the conquering power of Jesus' life was demonstrated by the empty tomb (Mark 16:6); (ii) by *water*, a reference to Jesus' baptism, at which God proclaimed who Jesus was (Mark 1:9–11); and (iii) by *blood*, a metaphor for Jesus' sacrificial death, when God again demonstrated that Jesus was his Son (Mark 15:37–39).

The second witness—what God has done in Christ John 6 : 35–51

As in the previous passage, what God does accords with what he says. Unlike us, he is consistent. Here are three of the greatest promises in Scripture: our salvation depends on God's work (44); our acceptance depends on his character (37); our surviving the course depends on his activity (40). Verse 51 refers to Christ's death. How does it give life to the world? Knowing that we are sinners is the first step in becoming a Christian; knowing that we are forgiven is the second. To doubt what God has done in your heart is to distrust what he has done in history.

The third witness—what God has done in your heart 1 John 3 : 11–24

The Bible is a supremely practical book. It's always probing for the spurious. We have cause to doubt our salvation if there is no change in us (14–18) if there is no love that grows. Becoming *and* being a Christian is a heart-changing experience and it's a gradual process. Don't make the mistake of thinking you're not a Christian because you're not yet perfect! But if you're making no progress to maturity, begin to doubt. Increasing dissatisfaction with yourself is a good sign; it means you are beginning to realize that his standards are much higher than you originally thought (19–24).

63

Growing

Feeding
John 6 : 25–40

Making progress as a Christian is hard work. (27). Growth is maintained by meditating on Christ's character, his words and works, and trusting him (29). Jesus himself is food that satisfies (35), and yet it is possible to see him and not partake, to look and not believe (36). Time must be set aside to come to him and feed. In our busy world spiritual undernourishment is increasingly common. Do not neglect yourself and starve. Take time today to assimilate these breathtaking words of Christ. Look for a promise to accept, a warning to heed and a truth to grasp.

Drinking
John 4 : 7–26

This famous story is packed full with meaning and the opportunity for personal application today is enormous. Note (i) the reversal of roles—it is not Jesus in need, but the woman (7–12); (ii) the contrast of provision—his supply is eternal (13, 15); (iii) the accuracy of Jesus' assessment—he knows her real situation; (iv) the gentleness of his ways (20–26). Worship now no longer requires a special place (20, 21), nor is it open to a particular people only (22). The requirements now are spiritual and moral (23, 24). An increasing thirst to worship the living God is satisfied by meeting Christ (25, 26).

Abiding
John 15 : 1–11

This eloquent picture of the Christian life is dramatic in its directness, inescapable in its meaning and straightforward in its demands. With a logic that cannot be defied the picture is gradually built up. Fruitfulness is a sign of belonging (2); increasing fruitfulness is the Father's work (1, 2). Dissociation spells disaster (4, 5) and destruction (6). Association with him means paying attention to his words (7). The favour of Father and Son rests only on those who obey (9, 10), and there is joy all round if these things are heeded (11). A healthy relationship leads to growth and joy unspeakable.

Understanding

Reading 1 Peter 1:22—2:3

Peter is writing to Christians to remind them of what has happened to them, and to exhort them to work out the consequences (22). Their new birth is not a passing phase but an indestructible fact (23–25), because the seed of God's word has a life and power which nothing can destroy. It was good news which they heard, understood and received (25). That's what made them Christians, and it was the same 'Word' which was to keep them Christians (2). Their appetite has been whetted (3). Are you increasingly hungry for the truth, to understand it and apply it?

Searching John 5:30–47

The witness to the identity of Jesus is impressive. John the Baptist's ministry had been explosive, his message direct, and his insistence that he simply pointed to Jesus uncompromising (33–35). The remarkable works of Jesus were eloquent testimony too (36). But the Jews' search contained the fatal refusal (40). It was a near miss, and all the more tragic for that. Even reading the Scriptures is a sterile exercise if we fail to come to the one of whom they speak, and his condemnation of those with false hopes is devastatingly contemporary (42–47).

Listening Luke 24:13–35

Of all the moving stories in Scripture this must be amongst the greatest. There is a ring of authenticity in the artless way in which it is told, with the disciples' sadness (17), their amazement at his ignorance of recent events (18), his patient explanation of the significance of those events (27), the meal and his identification (31) and the need for immediate action (33). Listening always comes before acting; being taught by Christ himself always leads to a burning heart (32) and we find it impossible to keep such new experiences to ourselves (35). Is that true of you?

Revealing

New life—hidden   Colossians 3 : 1–11

The Christian's changed status (1) results in a complete
reorientation (1, 2). So dramatic is this change that Paul
describes it as a matter of dying, and says that our new life is
hidden from the world (3). No-one will know for certain that
you belong to Christ until he returns and all is revealed (4).
Here and now, however, there are necessary objective
changes which are the tell-tale marks of this hidden new
life—purity of heart (5) leading to purity of relationships (8,
9) and a demolition of old barriers (11).

New life—exposed   Acts 8 : 26–40

This story of an educated man looking for the truth teaches
us that the person who understands the good news about
Christ and accepts him and his teaching goes on to
demonstrate publicly his new-found allegiance. Baptism is
the mark of belonging to Christ; it is a symbol of the change
of heart. It does not make you a Christian, but it is the
characteristic sign of a believing heart. It is the public act
which exposes your private transaction with God. If your
new relationship is still a secret, make sure that the world
gets to know about it now.

New life—sustained   1 Corinthians 11 : 23–26

Christ's death is central to the Christian life. We do not know
how the disciples understood these words at the time they
were spoken, but we do know how the early church inter-
preted them subsequently. Look up 1 Peter 2:24 and 3:18.
What is the unique achievement of Jesus' death? Why do
we need to remember it today? The bread and wine are symbolic—to help us remember (24, 25) that forgiveness can be
obtained nowhere else. By partaking we demonstrate our
contemporary need of what he has obtained for us, and
proclaim to the world what he has done (26). Thank him
afresh.

Obeying

An old, old principle   Exodus 19 : 1–6
In the last few studies we have seen the need of new understanding. A further indispensable part of being a Christian
is real obedience. Our faith is not of academic interest only
but has practical implications which cannot safely be ignored; this is because we are dealing with a real God and
not one which we have made up. The whole exodus story is
a thrilling account of God's dealings with his people and this
excerpt highlights the conditions for success (5). Past victories are no guarantee of future blessing (4), only obedience
will secure that (5).

Sure foundations   Matthew 7 : 21–29
Jesus endorses the theme of the Old Testament. Those who
blandly say that they live by the Sermon on the Mount can't
have read it very carefully or seen the significance of its
ending, which describes a house tumbling like a pack of
cards—a life in ruins. And the ruined life is one where
obedience is absent (21, 26). Belief which doesn't lead to
action is spurious (26) and will eventually be shown to be so
(27); listening and obeying is a combination which nothing
can shake (24, 25). Is your faith more than words?

Which master will you have?   Romans 6 : 12–23
This is the middle of a great passage where Paul is arguing
that Christian freedom is not an excuse for licence. Our liber-
ty is not one *from* obeying Christ but *for* obeying him. We
have been made free from serving and obeying sin (12–14)
and are now able to enjoy the freedom of serving him (17,
18). And the joy of it all is that whereas our previous service
of sin and self spelt death (21) the service of our new master
spells life (22). We cannot avoid having a master—which is
it to be? Notice the force of verse 19—there's a *process* in
one direction or the other.

Enjoying

Life John 10:1–18

This famous metaphor explodes two popular myths—one, that we can make our own way in the world successfully, and two, that becoming a Christian is signing our death warrant. Certainly the world still believes both myths. It thinks that we need no shepherd and fails to realize that the spurious exists (5, 10, 12, 13), offering life but bringing death (10), claiming good motives but possessing none (12). In contrast, Christ has demonstrated his love for us (15) and through his death he brings us life. Look up Luke 4:16–21 for Jesus' description of his mission.

Freedom John 8:31–38

The world thinks that the Christian is imprisoned in religion, but those who do belong to Christ know that only they are truly free (32). Why? What is the worst slavery in the world (34)? Did you notice what the requirements were for your continued freedom (31)? The controversy is a salutary one for these Jews did indeed have a privileged position, but through the pride in their pedigree they had lost their grasp on the things that really mattered (33, 34) and were busy attempting to extinguish God's contemporary revelation (37). Our freedom needs jealous guarding (34).

Peace Philippians 4:1–7

Peace is an increasingly scarce and precious commodity. The peace which the world offers is obtained by producing tranquil surroundings. In contrast, Christian peace is internal. It passes all understanding, since it doesn't depend on outward circumstances (7). Rejoicing is only sensible if you believe the Lord to be at hand (5) and ceasing to be anxious is possible only if you know something of prayer and thanksgiving (6). Joy and peace are the products of confidence in God and the privileged possession of those who trust in him.

Memorizing verses

The subject of 'memory' is an exciting biblical theme, and it is well worth doing a study on the word 'remember'. Life is too busy to be continually referring back to the textbook every minute. We don't think much of a doctor who, at the scene of an accident, has to consult his books before he acts.

Similarly, to say that you are obeying and applying God's Word to your life when you don't know what it says is nothing but patent nonsense (John 14:21).

There are many helps and aids, such as those produced by the Navigators, the Crusaders Union and the Scripture Union.* Use one to get you started and then devise your own.

Take note of the following:

Be systematic	Unless you are, it will not get done!
Be adventurous	There is no reason why you should not learn chapters or even whole letters. A time may come when the Bible is taken away from us.
Be outgoing	Though Scripture memorization has great value in temptation (Psalm 119:9), guidance (Psalm 119:105) and the personal side of the Christian life, it is also crucial to our proclamation and defence of the gospel (1 Peter 3:15).
Be patient	It is very hard work. Don't give up, especially at the beginning, because it does get easier with practice.
Be observant	Every situation in which we find ourselves has a scripture which has some bearing on it. Work from the life situation to the Bible as well as the other way around.

*The Navigators, Tregaron House, 27 High Street, New Malden, Surrey KT3 4BY; the Crusaders Union, 2 Romeland Hill, St Albans, Herts, AL3 4GT; the Scripture Union, 47 Marylebone Lane, London W1M 6AX.

Praying

A divine pattern   Luke 11:1-13

Children want to talk with their father. Notice how the disciples were inspired by Jesus' example (1, 2). There's
nothing like seeing and hearing someone else at prayer for
catching the infectious joy and reality of it all. The pattern is
God's concerns first, followed by our neighbour and then
ourselves (2-4). It contains statements and requests and
ranges from forgiveness of sin to daily bread. What is the
point of the story (5-13)? Do you talk to God as if he were a
miserly donor? Do you thank him for the good gifts you
receive and what do you ask for?

A human contrast   Luke 18:1-8

Like the exam question, this parable is to 'compare and contrast'. Don't miss the situation in which the story is told (1),
for it remains contemporary and relevant today. If you think
God is like Scrooge you soon lose heart and give up, but
Jesus says that his Father is very far removed from such a
figure. The contrast is enormous; there is no comparison.
Why then 'unanswered prayer'? The passage hints that our
timing may not be the same as his (7, 8).

Attitudes which matter   Luke 18:9-14

Prayer must begin on our knees, metaphorically if not literally, for there is nothing that ensures that our prayers are unanswered more than a self-righteous spirit (9)—a further
reason to add to those above. Make a list of the contrasting
features of the two men and identify your own position.
Does your humility extend to when you are alone with God?
The Pharisee's thoughts were all in terms of comparison
with other people. If you eradicate all such thought when you
are alone with God, your attitude in the rush and bustle of
life will be transformed too. The justified person dwells on
God's mercy (13, 14).

Confessing

The joy in heaven
Luke 15 : 1–10
Of the many things which mark the new people, confession and repentance are indispensable features, and the idea remains as unpopular with us today as it did with the Pharisees (1, 2). Jesus' presence with the disreputable was not to condone their activities but to change them, and change can come only when we admit that we are lost (3, 6, 8, 9). The new people are those who have acknowledged that fact and had a change of heart and direction, an essential feature of repentance (7, 10). Failure to repent means that heaven remains silent and that people remain lost.

Our initiative and his
Luke 15 : 11–24
A Christian immediately identifies with this story, for it describes his own situation. It vividly describes a gradual realization of being in the wrong place and of being meant for something better (17), of the need to make a personal apology (18, 21), and how he was welcomed as a son and not a servant (22–24). It is a perfect illustration of the fact that there can be no family party without the son's turning back home, and yet the Father's love is not only waiting but coming to meet him (20). There is no joy, however, unless we come to our senses (17).

Reality and self-deception
1 John 1 : 5–10
John solemnly warns us that God's purity is not a myth or a figment of our imagination (5) and that the way we talk may simply indicate that we're living in cloud cuckoo land (6). It is only as our sin comes out from the dark corners of our self-deception into the cold light of day that it can be dealt with (7). To be dealt with it must be exposed. Hiding the truth—even from ourselves (8)—gets us nowhere, but we can be sure that frank exposure will lead to forgiveness and cleansing (9).

Belonging

A body   1 Corinthians 12 : 12–26

A solitary Christian is a contradiction in terms (12, 14). We are related to one another because we share our new life in Christ: old divisions are irrelevant (13). The different members of the church are neither dispensable nor identical (14–21) but are complementary; and effective relationships with one another derive from a common obedience to the Lord, the head. Identification with your local part of his body is vital to life, and if its expression in the church round the corner seems weak, then there is special reason to join it (22–25)! Your allegiance to Christ demands allegiance to his people.

A building   1 Peter 2 : 1–10

God is constructing a building in which he lives. It is not yet complete but in his purposes you are a valuable addition. Its foundation is especially precious to him (4) and the rest of the building is acceptable on Christ's account (5). The building may not look much in the world's eyes, but everyone who is part of it will be unashamed at the end of the day (6). Those who have avoided obedience will find the cornerstone a stumbling-block (7, 8). What is the starting-point (10) and the purpose of the building?

Christ's headship   Ephesians 4 : 1–16

Belonging to this new community is demanding (1–3), but one's membership is secured by the things we hold in common (4–6). The one Lord (7) gives different gifts (11) for one purpose (12). Maturity is measured by increasing likeness to Christ (13) and growing ability to recognize false teaching (4). Note that the growth is mutually attained and is not just an individual affair (15, 16). Learning from one another (14), exhorting one another (1), being honest with one another (15)—these are God's appointed ways to grow, and to neglect one another is to disobey the head.

Service

Living for him   2 Corinthians 5 : 14–21

In the last three studies we have seen that being a Christian
is to live a radiantly joyful and free life. Such life comes from
finding the purpose for which we were made—and therein
lies the paradox, for we were made not primarily for
ourselves but for God, and secondarily for our neighbour. We
find ourselves in service. One of the purposes of Christ's
death was to transform our self-service into living for
him—which verse says that? Look it up, and meditate on its
significance for you. Pray that you may live for him today.

Living for others   Luke 10 : 29–37

This story is deceptively well known; don't miss the crucial
points. What question is Jesus answering (29)? Write down
what you think his answer is. Make sure that you apply the
following questions to your life: (i) What obvious need finds
me passing by on the other side (31, 32)? (ii) Is my religion a
cloak for complacency and self-satisfaction (31, 32)? (iii)
Does my care extend to the long term (35)? What other
parables and teaching of Jesus illustrate this theme of service for others? (Why not make an extra study of this theme?)
Your greatest service to anyone is to introduce them to Christ
(John 1:45).

Using ourselves   Luke 19 : 11–27

Like so many of Jesus' parables this one is uncomfortably
near to home, for though its setting is one of eternal realities
(11, 15, 26, 27) its implications are very down to earth. The
people felt that God was absent but about to return (11) and
Jesus' story acknowledges that they are right. The story
turns on the fact that what they have is not their own, and
that the returning King will demand an account of what use
they have made of his gifts (15). Faithfulness brings its
reward (17, 19). Infidelity brings its reward (24, 26). What
profit are you to the King?

Temptation

The devil's questions (i)   Genesis 3:1-21

One of the characteristic marks of the new people is that they become increasingly conscious of temptation and failure. They are increasingly able to identify with this story and they cannot regard the devil as mythical, because they have met him. He is the chief purveyor of doubt (1) and lies (4) and his methods are indeed subtle (1, 5). Following his advice does make us ashamed in God's presence (8), and obeying him does have practical consequences (14–19). The chapter is an accurate account of cosmic realities —temptation is real, falling is real, displeasing God is real.

The devil's questions (ii)   Matthew 4:1-11

There are three pivotal points in the history of man; his creation, his fall and his redemption. In Adam the devil won the day, in Christ the heavenly Father prevailed. For Christ the temptation was real (1), at an awkward time (2) and having some very cogent arguments in its favour—why not prove what you know unmistakably to be true (3, 6)? It is important to grasp that being tempted does not displease God; falling does. Jesus triumphed because he knew falsity when he saw it, and that was because he knew the Scriptures. To withstand temptation—study and apply.

The devil's object   2 Corinthians 11:1-6

The Corinthian church was a very ebullient one, but judging from Paul's two letters it was an immature one. In this passage he warns them of Satan's activity—what form it will take (4) and what it seeks to achieve (3). Notice his first point of attack—thoughts, for thoughts always precede action. The sincerity and purity of our devotion to Christ is a matter of the mind, and Satan's strategy is a deflecting one which may use human agency (4) to focus attention on a fabricated Jesus or a counterfeit gospel. The truth, however, is plain.

Fighting

A test
James 1 : 2–15

Though the Christian life is one of joy, it is not without trials and hardship. If your life is without difficulty it probably isn't the real Christian life; there has probably been compromise along the way. A happy disposition towards trial is possible only when its purpose is in view (3) and its end in sight (4, 12). Double-mindedness in such a situation is a fatal disease (7, 8). Ask yourself today whether your pursuits are after things that will last or things that will fade away (11). Can you discern the pattern of verses 14, 15 in yourself?

A battle
Ephesians 6 : 10–20

This war in which the new people are engaged is a spiritual one (12) against a cunning enemy (11) and weapons of both attack and defence are vital both for self-preservation (13) and to defeat the enemy. Truth and righteousness are unfailing protection (14), knowing the gospel makes movement possible (15) and simple trust in God is ample defence (16). To understand the helmet see subsequent studies (pp. 97 ff.). God's word to us (17) makes attack possible (are you beginning to love his Word and memorize it?), and our words to God make endurance possible (18).

A victory
Mark 13 : 1–13

It is not only James and Paul who warn us about the spurious but Jesus himself (5, 6). His teaching here is about a period of general distress (7, 8) and of particular distress for those who claim to be Christians (9–13). At the moment, in the West, persecution is limited; but you should know that in our own generation many face trial, torture and death. What are you prepared to do for his sake (9, 13)? Jesus brings division even in families (12), but endurance of even such a trial as this will be vindicated (13). Victory is secure.

Working

A faith that works (i) Matthew 25 : 31–46

Jesus stands against all 'pie-in-the-sky' religion that is divorced from practical reality. He also stands against the modern cynic who regards spiritual realities as mythical. This parable is a frightening illustration of these facts. There will be a day when he comes with his angels (31) and there will be a separation (32). There will be a happy ending for some (34) and an awful ending for others (41, 46) and the distinction will be based on what we have done to Christ—the Christ whose teaching has sharp edges, and not a 'religious' Christ of our imagination.

A faith that works (ii) James 2 : 14–26

James follows the teaching of his master and identifies a living and effective faith as one that works. Faith that has no practical results is no faith at all (17). Make a list today of the areas in your life which have been transformed since you came to faith in Christ. Is there a practical area (15, 16)? The Old Testament characters pleased God and were 'justified' (made fit for his presence) not because of what they said but because of what they did (21, 23, 25). The new people of God are new on the outside as well as the inside.

A faith that works (iii) 2 Thessalonians 3 : 6–12

For many young Christians, the good news that they have just grasped for the first time is so good and new that it fills the horizon to the exclusion of their proper responsibilities and duties. True, the gospel remains the most important thing in the world, but its proclamation is no excuse for idleness (6) and no cause for sponging (8). The real thing always produces a worker (7), fully aware of practical realities.

You may have your head in the clouds, but Paul's remedy is to bring you down to your earthly stomach (10)!

Resting

Divine pattern
Genesis 1:26—2:3

If idleness is not Christian, neither is working without a regular break and rest. We just don't function as God intended if we neglect a regular time of rest and refreshment, and the Genesis account tells us why things are this way. It is because we are made in his image (26, 27), and like him (2) we must have a time when our work is finished (3). His dominion over the earth in creating it did not preclude his need of rest, and neither does our delegated dominion (28–30) evade our need to recuperate. Work out your rest pattern.

Rigid interpretation
Luke 6:1-11

Keeping the sabbath holy is part of God's law (Exodus 20:1-17). The Pharisaic interpretations had laid down hundreds of rules about what you could or couldn't do on the sabbath, and in so doing had lost sight of its original purpose. Jesus cites David as someone who wasn't bound by tradition in the face of obvious necessity (3, 4) and Jesus himself illustrates this remorseless logic by healing on the sabbath (10). God's command to rest does not rule out meeting practical needs. How can you work out this principle in your own situation?

Contemporary principle
Exodus 20:8-11

The first word of this command is very significant. Our disobedience is often not so much rank rebellion as sheer neglect, and it is our poor *memories* that are the cause of God's displeasure. Make sure that you are not quietly forgetting this command. Notice that it is in two parts: negative, no work on one day; positive, hard work on the others (9). Are you hard at it on the working days, or is that part of the principle to which you only vaguely adhere? Does the principle extend to people around you (10)?

Giving

Sacrificially   Mark 12 : 38–44

The new people in Christ are those who know that all that
they have is a gift from God. Their whole way of thinking is
dominated by the fact that whatever they possess, whether
time, money, talents, a body, or salvation, is all a gift from
God—owned by him and not them. What we used to value
highly (38–40) is seen to be of small importance, and we
gradually learn to slacken our grasp on what we once
thought it important to keep. What we can give varies
according to what we have been given (Luke 12:48), and
God requires us to be like him—sacrificially generous.

Cheerfully   2 Corinthians 9 : 5–15

It is a quite extraordinary paradox, which needs to be learnt
by every generation and especially by ours, that the cheerful
giver will be blessed beyond his wildest dreams. Any enterprise depends on what you put into it (6) and Paul requires
us to make a sober calculation (7). Have you done that yet?
You ought to make a study of both the biblical principles and
your bank balance. Note the several results of generosity
(11–14). You will please God and bring him glory by your
giving, but don't think you can buy your way into heaven—he
owns it!

Regularly   1 Corinthians 16 : 1–9

If our chief sin in giving money is to be tight-fisted, a very
close second is our irregularity. If by nature we were spon-
taneous givers, verse 2 would be unnecessary, but the truth
is that we need a routine to discipline us to give the barest
minimum! Note that the timing is to be regular but the
amount is to fluctuate according to circumstances. Often
today there is a wide-open door for effective work (9) but
one of the many adversaries is the ill-discipline of the Christian giver. Have you worked it out yet? If so, have you
revised it recently?

III
Varied solids:

a way in to
the variety of Bible
study possibilities

Many Christians find that when they have been studying the Bible for a year or so, their studies become stereotyped and therefore less fruitful than they could be. This may be because they have never seen how else to approach it, or have only ever used one kind of study aid. The intention of this section is to give examples of the various ways one can approach the Bible, digging out a doctrine or theme, a word or character; skipping fast over large areas, or slowing right down and thinking repeatedly about the same passage seen from different angles. We have tried to make a selection of subjects and passages from various parts of the Bible so that your over-all knowledge of its teaching accumulates as you go.

Aids to Bible study

Aids to Bible study are not unspiritual (after all, God gave us the Bible itself as an aid to knowing him, and it acknowledges the need for help in understanding what it says (Acts 8:30, 31; Nehemiah 8:8)). Besides public teachers, God has provided through the work of gifted people many valuable tools for mining the treasures in his Word. Provided that we do not let them become a substitute for the Bible itself, such aids can shed additional light on the way and may help us to avoid a wrong turning. There are three main kinds:

1 There are practical things which make us more efficient or help us to concentrate. For instance, pencil and notebook help to focus attention and enable us to record and review truths we have learnt.

2 Some books have been compiled to help us get hold of what is already in the Bible without further addition or comment. One such is the concordance, which lists many occurrences of the same word (see p. 125); a topical Bible will print out all the passages on a given theme. Other books give cross references from verse to verse—*The treasury of Scripture knowledge* offers half a million! These books indicate by *usage* what a word means, and highlight the meaning of the Bible as a whole on a particular subject. So long as you keep each text in context, this method of study can enrich and balance your understanding and excite you with the unity of God's Word.

3 Other aids, like this book, set out to give additional information or help the reader to interpret the passage. Commentaries, Bible dictionaries and atlases, study guides and systematic theologies all aim to bring knowledge and insight from history, geography, contemporary life or Scripture itself to bear on your passage. They vary widely in usefulness, accuracy and theological slant, and advice should be taken; but used wisely they can open up large new vistas of truth.

1. The church: a topical study

What the church is

A body   1 Corinthians 12 : 12–27
Paul is using an extended metaphor to teach us how individuals in the church should relate to one another. What is the basis of unity of the body of Christ? How do parts of a human body differ—in function or importance? What does the passage have to say about jealousy of another's spiritual gifts? About assuming that someone in the church is dispensable? Which parts of the body of Christ might be considered 'inferior'? How are we to treat such persons?

A new temple/a new family   Ephesians 2 : 17–22
Here the apostle mixes his metaphors slightly, referring to the church first as the 'household' of God and then, by implication, as the 'house' of God. Does verse 18 give you any clue as to the difference between an alien and a member of God's household? How do we use the privilege? How is Jesus, the cornerstone, related to the rest of the building? Notice that God does not live inside this building but in the very building blocks. From the passage, how would you expect the church to grow (21) or be built up (22)? This temple is holy (21). What should that mean for the church?

A bride   Ephesians 5 : 21–33
This analogy shows how Jesus is the perfect husband and how the church should be a submissive bride. Notice that the passage assumes that the church is the body of Christ (23, 29). How does Jesus show his love for the church? What does it mean in practice for the church to submit to Christ (think about verse 23)? What is the future event for which Christ is preparing his bride? What will the church be like then? Submission to Christ is essential if this process is to be completed. Ask God to reveal to you any of your rebellion.

Don't neglect the teaching on the marriage relationship.

What the church does

Getting together Acts 2 : 41–47

Luke gives us a description of the activities of the earliest congregation of Christian believers. Notice who was involved (41, 47). List the specific activities in which they were engaged, and then notice what might be called the results or by-products. For instance, fellowship (42) literally means 'sharing' or 'participation'. Verses 44 and 45 describe one way this was manifested. How do the working of God and the activities of people in the church inter-relate? The idea behind 'devoted' (42) is that of steady continuation. Are you continually and regularly giving yourself to the activities mentioned in this verse?

Proclamation 1 Peter 2 : 9–17

This passage is about verbal and visual communication of the message of salvation. Our corporate identity in Christ is the basis for the proclamation and life-style which Peter calls for. How are we described in the passage? Philippians 3:20 may help put this together into one idea. How is our proclamation related to our status? Does citizenship in God's kingdom allow us to disregard the earthly kingdom of which we are citizens? Why or why not (13)? What are some criticisms of the church which could be corrected by our obeying the commands given in this passage?

Service Galatians 6 : 1–10

In this passage, the apostle Paul first sets out some specific ways in which we can serve one another in the church, and then widens the application to include those outside. List the specific ways we can serve our brothers and sisters in Christ. What is the inherent danger in trying to restore a brother? How far does the duty of supporting other Christians imply that others are responsible for me? This is a good example of how Scripture has built-in guards against being twisted to shift responsibility to others.

How is 'sowing to the Spirit' related to good deeds? Verse 10 speaks of opportunity. What opportunities do you have to do good deeds?

What the church has

Gifts
1 Corinthians 12 : 1–11

This section is addressed to a local assembly where the exercise of spiritual gifts had got out of perspective. Paul tries to replace misunderstanding with positive teaching.

What are spiritual gifts, according to verse 7? What are they for? The words 'service' (5) and 'working' (6) remind us that gifts are not exercised by putting the mind in neutral but by getting on with the hard work of service in whatever way God wants to use us. Since gifts are for the upbuilding of others, others are often best able to tell us what gifts we have. Notice who gives the gifts and to whom they are given. Ask God to help you to discover your spiritual gifts and look for ways to serve others. Your gifts will become evident in the way God blesses the efforts and inspires you to do the works.

Blessings
Ephesians 1 : 3–10

The Greek word for 'to bless' means 'to speak well of', and this passage reminds us of all the good things God has spoken or done where we are concerned. Our natural response is to speak well of him (3). List the good things we have 'in Christ' that are mentioned in these verses. 'In heavenly places' does not mean that these things are inaccessible or that we must wait until death to receive them, but rather that we already have them because Jesus has been exalted to the heavenly places and we are 'in him'. Think though how you can put to use these good things God has given. Thank him for the richness of his grace.

A hope
Titus 2 : 11–14

This passage is one of many which remind us that the return of Jesus should be a powerful motivation to godliness. How is Jesus described in the passage? What is the purpose of his first coming? His second? What difference in the two appearances is implied in verse 13? What do we do while we are waiting?

2. Joseph and the providence of God: a character study

Genesis 37–50

The story of Joseph is a fascinating one. To read it as a whole is instructive, for the striking thing about it is that the central character is not Joseph! However hard we try to make Joseph the centre of attention, we are thwarted at every turn. It is God who holds the centre of the stage. It is he who demands consideration. It is he who is behind it all, who is in it all and working through it all. To be sure, we have much to learn about the man God uses, but in looking at the human character, don't miss the divine one. It is supremely a story about God's providential care, and we stand in great need of recovering the certainty that he has not lost control. So let's learn from God's dealing with Joseph that though circumstances may change, God does not.

The election of God 37 : 1–36

Right from the start we recognize this as a story about real people: Jacob, a tiresome old man; his children, unsavoury characters, with Joseph a sneak (2) and a fool (5–9). We learn (1) that God's choices cannot be questioned—Joseph was part of a bigger plan whether he liked it or not (Genesis 15:13 predicts events that began to take place in Joseph's life-time); (ii) that God's purposes can't be thwarted in spite of Joseph's indiscretion and folly, and (iii) that God's ways and means can't be excelled—Joseph was being spoilt by his father and corrupted by his brothers, so he is taken away from them. God is the controlling reality; do you welcome that?

The plan of God   39 : 1–23

(i) *Triumph* (1–6): here is a wonderful success story, with a human side (a job well done, 4), and a divine side (2, 3, 5). (ii) *Temptation* (6–18) is often the sequel to triumph. Joseph's reaction is model: there are at least five key features; what are they? (iii) *Tragedy* (19–23): in prison, Joseph first experienced God's steadfast love (21), and he knew God's favour in unfavourable circumstances (22). The lesson is a crucial one to learn; Joseph was who he was whether in Potiphar's house or Pharaoh's court. His character did not change with the circumstances.

The interpreter of God   40 : 1–23

Nothing happens by mistake. Joseph is being prepared by tribulation and suffering. You must let your imagination get into the story—two years is a long time (41:1) and the successful interpretation must have given a glimmer of hope (14) only to be dashed to pieces (23). The school of suffering has excellent results but nobody enjoys going through it. It must have seemed as if not only had the butler forgotten him but God had too! Providential care is often seen only in retrospect (which was why the story was written—so that we can learn from it). The prison experiences are to teach us to trust him (Psalm 105:16–22).

The gift of God   41 : 1–57

Why was Joseph so eminently successful in the pathway God chose? (i) His loyalty. Everything he did was done in relation to God; there is quite an extraordinary emphasis on it in the story (39:9, 41:16, 25, 28, 32, 51, 52). (ii) His energy. Everything he did was done with thoroughness and efficiency (46–49). God gave two great blessings, seen in the names of the children. Negatively (51), God enabled him to look back on the past and forget all the bitterness, and positively (52), God gave him fulfilment in the difficult place. God's purpose is always to make us fruitful.

The guidance of God 42:1-38

The insight that this narrative gives us on the matter of guidance should destroy our hang-ups for ever. Do you see how God's will gets done despite the obstacles—the old man's unwillingness (38, compare 15:13) and the sons' unworthiness (4, their father couldn't trust them)? Jacob was a rogue; ponder on the references to the 'God of Jacob' (*e.g.* Psalm 20:1; 46:7; Luke 20:37). They tell us that he is a God of grace who has the power and the patience to deal with such unpromising material. If God can guide such a man, can he not guide you?

The mercy of God 43:1-34

God's great purpose is to make his people holy. He knows that if he gives them success it usually goes to their head. How to bless them without spoiling them is his dilemma, which he resolves by bringing them to their destination along circuitous and uncomfortable routes (*e.g.* Deuteronomy 8:2). Trials and tribulations are part of his mercy and love—for Joseph, sorrow, hunger, imprisonment; for the brothers, fear, hunger, imprisonment; and for Jacob, loss of Joseph and Benjamin. Perhaps we go through difficulties because God can't trust us with much without our becoming unteachable.

Guilt before God 44:1-34

Joseph tests his brothers to see if they are the same as before. He carefully engineers the situation so that it is parallel to the one when he himself was ditched by them—the favourite being the youngest (43:33, 34) and possessing something the others lacked (12). But the brothers had changed. Judah pleads for Benjamin (18) and there is unanimity (13), frankness and constancy (16) now. Why the change? Fear has entered them (42:21, 28). Inexplicable situations lead to fear which turns us to God. Look up Colossians 1:28; Philippians 2:12; 2 Corinthians 7:1 and Psalm 2:11, 12.

The mission of God   45:1–28

Joseph was completely free of all rancour and bitterness, an amazing fact stemming from his sense of being involved in the much larger plan of God, something much bigger than the little details and events. Joseph relates to God all the time (5, 7, 8, 9). Human reconciliation is possible when we have such an attitude and focus. This doesn't, however, make him 'infallible' (48:17–19), inhuman (2, 3—to see things spiritually is to see them humanly), or any less shrewd (22, 23, 26—he is aware of his father's settled scepticism). God is for ever re-creating people and relationships.

The promises of God   46:1–34

God's promise to Jacob is a reiteration of the Old Testament covenant (12:1–3; 15:13–16). The idea of 'covenant' is a key biblical idea and you should do a special study on it. The relation between God and us begins with his promises, which is very striking since there is no verb or noun in Hebrew for 'promise'. It's not needed! When God speaks, that's sufficient. His speech is an announcement of his purpose, unlike ours so often. Note that he takes the initiative (2); compare the pagan order where man takes the initiative and seek to manipulate God. God is in this human story (28–34).

The wisdom of God   47:1–31

The whole story is full of surprises. In this chapter we see a great reversal of fortunes (2–27) with extraordinary generosity from Pharaoh. Don't miss the unexpected order of who gives the blessing in verse 7. Though one sees the shrewdness of Joseph (14–26), one senses that the wisdom belongs to God. It is his plan which is being unfolded. This concept is clean contrary to modern man's thinking; we want to have God taped, a puppet on a string, dancing to man's tune. But God will not be reduced to such proportions, and Joseph knows it.

The free grace of God   48 : 1–22

God's freedom and choice are uppermost in this study; he alone is free to do what he wants and he is the God of grace showing love and mercy to those who don't deserve it. It is very interesting to see how Jacob came to learn submission to such sovereign grace, for his name means 'cheat' (27:36). There was sorrow, trial and difficulty (31:36–42; 47:9; 48:7) and yet, in looking back, he sees the hand of God. It remains true that scheming without trusting leads to self-pity.

The blessing of God   49 : 1–33

In one sense, Christians lead a 'double life'; we are 'in the world' but 'part of heaven' (*e.g.* Colossians 1:2—the saints are 'in Colossae' and also 'in Christ'). Similarly with Joseph; he lived 'in God' in very varied circumstances—the pit, the prison, Pharaoh's palace—and because of this his life was fruitful. He consistently put God first and he constantly lived for others. He knew tribulation (23), but his character was made and not marred by it. A fruitful life is the inheritance of every Christian, because God has promised it to those who trust him. What are the rules (Psalm 1; John 15)?

The good purposes of God   50 : 1–26

Two magnificent features of Joseph are highlighted here. First, his godliness. In a position to be a tyrant (15), his reaction is not anger, nor even condescension, but tears. He left all righting of wrongs to God (19); vengeance was God's business (Romans 12:19), and he had learnt to leave it with God. He saw God's providential ordering in everything (20), which yet does not excuse Joseph from practical action (2). Second, Joseph's hope. As he looked back at God's loyalty to him, his confidence was in God for greater blessings in the future. Trust brings serenity.

88

3. Joys and problems in 1 Thessalonians: studying a whole epistle

Enthusiasm

chapter 1

Paul's visit to Thessalonica, the flourishing and strategic capital of the province of Macedonia, appears in Acts 17. Leaving in haste he sent Timothy back from Athens for news, and he caught up with a dispirited Paul at Corinth. The news encouraged Paul greatly and he wrote this letter from there in about AD 50. It is one of the earliest parts of the New Testament, and is full of the atmosphere and concerns of those days. Can you list the specific things for which he was grateful? How far—and why—are faith, love and hope the hallmarks of a Christian?

Example

2:1–12

Paul's reputation seems to have come under fire from opponents in Thessalonica; fraudulent wandering preachers were numerous and this would be a good line to unsettle his converts. Paul replies for Timothy and Silas (=Silvanus, 1:1) as well as himself. The facts spoke for themselves. They had not been having an easy time (the events in Philippi are recorded in Acts 16:11–40), they had worked hard, and their motives were transparently right. What apostolic rights (6) did Paul forgo? What do the twin pictures of nurse and father suggest? How might we fall into the traps Paul avoided?

Experience

2:13–3:10

This apparently 'chatty' section contains some knotty problems and some useful teaching and information. For instance, how can we tell the difference between the word of men and the word of God (13)? Has God's wrath really fallen on the Jews (16)? How can Satan hinder God's work (18)? Try to gather up the various comments on (i) the place of persecution, (ii) the activity of Satan, (iii) the character of Timothy. There is also more here about Paul the pastor—what do we learn from it for ourselves?

Exhortation 3:11–4:12

God's will is our sanctification: but what is that? Find out the meaning of the word and work out its implications in practice today (see pp. 112 f.). There is a link between the positive love which Christians have for each other, and the negative refusal to hurt each other which immorality and idleness would cause. What, if any, is the difference between the love Christians have for each other and their love for people in general (3:12)? Does Paul really help us on how to 'take a wife' (or husband) for oneself? What do verses 11 and 12 of chapter 4 have to do with love of the brethren?

Explanation 4:13–5:11

Some of the idleness referred to previously was caused by the idea that Christ's return was imminent. When, in fact, does Paul say that it will take place? Naturally those who expected Christ's return immediately were disturbed when some fellow Christians died before it happened. Did this mean that the Lord had let them down, or that Paul had misled them, or that their friends would miss the joy of that day? Paul puts them right; how, exactly? Could you speak on this at a funeral, in obedience to verse 18? How else are Christians to behave while waiting for Christ's return (chapter 5)?

Encouragement 5:12–28

Are verses 12 and 13 out of date? Is there any basis for this view of authority in the churches, and if so, what difference should it make to your own fellowship? Paul rattles off advice here as if the piece of papyrus is running out! Can you select two of his commands which apply closely to yourself, and pray them over thoroughly? How do we go about quenching the Spirit—and what might happen if we didn't? What, in the context, is the 'everything' we are to test? How much of all this is God's work (23), and how much is ours?

Meditation

What is meditation? In recent years many people have become involved in mystical techniques, often related to certain eastern religions. This may involve thought on some theme or virtue, but on the whole it is an internal search for peace or spiritual experience (see *God and the gurus* by R. D. Clements, IVP).

Christian meditation differs in several ways. It relates to a real and personal God of specific moral character, and is a matter not of emptying my mind but of filling it with truth in order to deepen my understanding, foster my relationship with God, move my behaviour into goodness, and fill my praying with meaning and joy. There may be spiritual experiences, but these will grow from and depend upon my contact with the truth as I find it in the living by his Spirit: for this reason a Christian's meditation is never far from prayer. Perhaps the best summary is in Paul's words, 'Whatever is true ... honourable ... just ... pure ... lovely ... gracious, if there is any excellence, ... anything worthy of praise, *think about these things.*' This is said (in Philippians 4:8) in the context of rejoicing, prayer, thanksgiving, peace of mind and practical action for good.

A Christian can helpfully meditate on beauty in art or nature, and on the beauty of Christ in works of painting, music or building; or he can sit in a field and reflect on aspects of Christ's life and influence. Any Christian's biography would open into meditation. But the deepest and most specific material on which to meditate will always be the inspired Scriptures of the Old and New Testaments, as they tell and explain the story of God's love. Such reflection needs time and requires the wisdom of learning verses and carrying them through the day; one Scots pastor used to say, 'Put that on your tongue and suck it like a sweetie'!

The Bible knows about meditation and breathes its atmosphere. In particular Psalms 1 and 119 discuss the value of meditating on God's words; think and pray through them sometime and you will get the idea.

4. Jesus' prayer for his people: a meditative study

Father and Son

John 17

There is sometimes great benefit in studying a passage over and over, perhaps every day for a week, looking each time at a different aspect of its message. If we do this with chapter 17 of John's Gospel, the natural starting-point is the relationship which Jesus displays between himself and his Father God. What do you learn about this relationship itself? What was the Father's original 'commission' to Jesus, and how has he fulfilled it? What particular needs does Jesus refer back to his Father in prayer, and how do you think he expected them to be met?

Jesus and company

John 17

The second significant relationship we can learn about here is the one between Jesus and his followers. What has he done for them, and how have they responded? How does Jesus view Judas and his role? What hopes does he have for their future, and what problems does he foresee? It will help to begin reading chapters 13–16 as background; these contain John's account of the Last Supper and the teaching Jesus gave on that evening. It is interesting to compare his ambitions for his followers (indicated in the prayer) with his instructions for achieving them (in the previous chapters).

Church and world

John 17

Jesus also enlarges on the relationship which will develop between his people and the world around them. Draw out the main factors in this relationship. What makes the people of Christ distinctive, and how far does this distinctiveness lead to separation from ordinary society? Putting it the other way round, in what ways should Christians be involved in the society round them, and what, if any, are the limits of such involvement? Think out what this implies for (i) your own career, (ii) local politics, (iii) international Christian concern for world development. How should we react to opposition?

Glory and honour
Broadly, the term 'glory' in the Bible suggests the awe-inspiring beauty, goodness and power associated with God's presence. You may like to do some homework (with a concordance and other study aids, see pp. 125, 151) on the meaning and use of the word. Then come back to John 17 and cull out the several references to glory in Jesus' prayer. What does he add to your understanding of glory? What light does the background of glory shed on this passage? How can we glorify someone—especially God? If possible, do a similar background study of 'joy', and try to explain verse 13.

Truth and love
Another cluster of words for attention; what does the Bible mean by the words for 'knowing', 'truth' and 'believing'? These obviously belong together; comb out and look at their use here. How far does the Bible think of knowing the truth in objective terms (*i.e.* as hard facts of reality) and how much as subjective (*i.e.* as facts of relationship or experience)? What are the implications for (i) church unity, and (ii) evangelism, both of which find a place in Jesus' prayer? If you can, look at the Bible's word 'love', and the way it links into these same themes here.

That you may believe
These days John's Gospel is mostly studied by Christians. It was, however, largely intended for outsiders, to convince them of Christianity (see chapter 20:30, 31). If you were not a Christian, what impression do you think you would get from this chapter? Would Jesus seem tougher or gentler than you thought, more remote or more accessible? Would Jesus' idea of his people compare with your experience of them? How might you react to verses 3, 9, 14, 18? As a Christian what would you choose to emphasize if a non-Christian friend came to you, confused by reading this passage?

5. Haggai: the Word of God in action

Background study Ezra 3 ; 4

In 536 BC Zerubbabel led about 50,000 Jews back to Jerusalem from captivity in Babylon. After sacrificing to the Lord they began to rebuild the temple (3:7–9). Why did the people have mixed emotions at this stage of rebuilding (3:11–13)? Opposition to any work of God can be external or internal. Look for two general tactics which the enemies of Judah used to halt reconstruction. Government structures can thwart God's purposes for a time, but notice 4:24. Who is in control ultimately?

The first vision Haggai 1 : 1–11

Darius was king of Persia about sixteen years later, when Haggai saw this vision. What seems to have happened in those intervening years? Notice how one excuse for not getting on with God's work has led to another. An external threat has become internal decay. Why does God draw attention to their circumstances? (19). The Jews' *priorities* were wrong. What was their excuse (2)? Take a few minutes to 'consider how you fare'. God may withhold blessing to force us to examine our priorities. When *is* the time to do God's work?

The effect of the first vision 1 : 12–15

From verse 12, why did all the people obey the words of Haggai? Fear of the Lord led to obedience. What two things did God do in response to that obedience (compare John 14:21)? Then what did the people do? Philippians 2:12, 13 is a New Testament statement of the same principle. Do God's commands seem too hard to accomplish? They are too hard for us alone. Praise God that he is at work within us.

94

Second vision: the glory of the temple   2:1-9

God drew attention to the comparative unimpressiveness of the new temple in order to teach a lesson. List God's instructions (4, 5) and his promises (5-9). God does not want us to trust in our own works. What are we to trust in? What is the appropriate response of one who is trusting God's promises, taking him at his word?

Third vision: uncleanness and blessing   2:10-19

The point of Haggai's riddle seems to be that contamination is contagious, while purity is not; a disease can be caught from an infected person but health can not be transmitted in the same way. What has been the effect of sin on national life? But notice that blessing, or lack of it, is more than simple cause and effect (17, 19). What was God's purpose in smiting? What did God do when Judah failed to get the message (1:1, 7)? Our generation seems slow to recognize that God is using difficult times to get our attention. What should we do?

Fourth vision: Zerubbabel the signet ring 2:20-23

Haggai again receives the word of the Lord. He is speaking about something soon to happen but which no doubt is intended to prefigure a greater event yet to come. Notice the expressions 'governor of Judah', 'that day', 'my servant', 'chosen'. They are all references to the Messiah or his return. Look at Hebrews 1:3. Does that description of Jesus help you to understand the signet ring image? As for the destruction of 'the kingdoms of the nations', read Revelation 11:15 and worship God!

The unity of Scripture

Not many books are written by some forty different people over a period of 1,500 years, spanning several different cultures. If they were, we should expect the individual contributions to display real differences in outlook, theme, accuracy and credibility, as well as in style and purpose. Now the Bible was written like that, but the expected result is not to be found—except perhaps by those whose expectations mould their conclusions. The whole book speaks of one God and his actions past, present and future, with and through one chosen people. Some people explain it away, some try to minimize it, but the Bible itself is not surprised by its manifest unity. Its pages say that the same Holy Spirit superintended the efforts of every writer so that the words which finally reached the papyrus were the ones God himself would use to convey this single message. That does not mean that God unloaded the whole message in the beginning and then just repeated himself; revelation was progressive and it became clearer and more complete as the appearance of Jesus approached.

Here are some of the important implications of the unity of Scripture:

1 It means that the Bible does not contradict itself. If it seems to do so, we have misinterpreted it.
2 God's character does not change. If the Old Testament picture of him seems to be incompatible with that in the New, remember that God is free to act as he chooses in order to demonstrate the various aspects of his single nature. Besides, this contrast has been greatly exaggerated; his love is not foreign to the Old Testament any more than his wrath is to the New.
3 No-one should ever base a doctrine on selected passages of Scripture while neglecting other passages which talk about the same subject.

6. Salvation: a doctrinal study

What is salvation?
Psalm 68 : 1–20

Salvation, in simplest terms, is deliverance. Go through this psalm and make a list of all those enemies, problems or evils from which God delivers people. God's nature is the key to salvation (20). What do we learn about God here which speaks of his ability to save? Salvation is not merely deliverance from evil, it is also the power to do good.

Why do we need salvation?
Psalm 51 : 1–17

David broke God's law by committing adultery and murder (2 Samuel 11, 12). Notice how that ruined his relationship with God (3, 4, 8, 9, 11, 14) so that even his religious practices became meaningless (16). What did David ask God for? Look for ten or eleven different requests. Why did David see his need (4)? What put him in a position to receive God's forgiveness (17)? What is the natural response of those who have seen their need and received God's salvation (13, 14)? Pray this psalm to God.

In what terms did God promise salvation?
Genesis 12 : 1–3, 17 : 1–9

God promised to save a people and to bless them and multiply them. In whom was the promise made (compare Galatians 3 : 6–9, 16)? What blessings were promised? On what conditions were these blessings to be received? How do you suppose Abraham could bless all the families of the earth (compare Matthew 1 : 1)? Look at Galatians 3 : 22 to see how we can obtain these promises.

What does salvation give us?
Jeremiah 31 : 10–14, 31–34

God had used captivity to judge his people. Now he promises restoration and hope. Verses 10–14 picture the abundant life. What is its basis in God's nature (12–14)? What words does Jeremiah use to describe the rescue itself? How is the new covenant the same as the old (the giving of the law on tablets of stone)? How is it different? How does God put this law within us?

How was salvation in Christ prefigured?

A 'type' is a model, a pre-production mock-up of the real thing. The Old Testament contains many *types* of Jesus—some human, some inanimate. Since there could be no perfect model of Jesus we should not press the details of biblical types but look for the point of similarity brought out by New Testament authors. Let's look at several of them. Study these at your own speed.

Jesus the lamb: Exodus 12:3–5, 12, 13, 46;
                                                              1 Corinthians 5:7

The lamb was to be without blemish. To what characteristic of Jesus does that correspond?

The burnt offering: Leviticus 1:2–5; Hebrews 10:4–10

Here we see the inadequacy of the symbols which pointed forward to the reality.

Cities of refuge: Numbers 35:6, 28; Hebrews 6:18

There are two analogies here. Notice how in Hebrews 6 the death of the high priest liberates the captive. Think about what it means to flee to Jesus from the *condemnation* of the law.

Manna: Exodus 16:11–15; John 6:32–35

Think of the ways in which Jesus is to us like manna was to the Israelites.

Moses: Deuteronomy 18:15–22; Acts 3:17–26

What do you learn about Jesus from the Deuteronomy passage? Explain why this passage for ever rules out the idea that Jesus was a simply a good moral teacher. If Jesus was wrong about his own identity, what should be our attitude toward him (Deuteronomy 18:20–22)? What if he is God's spokesman (18, 19)? How do we qualify to receive the blessing God offers in Jesus (Acts 3:19, 26)?

How was salvation provided?

In Jesus the eternal God–Man: Matthew 1:18–23

Everything about him is consistent with that fact. It may help you to know that a betrothed couple had all the legal advantages of marriage even though they had not consummated it physically. Go through this passage carefully to discover everything you can about Jesus: names, titles, parentage, calling. 'Jesus' or 'Yeshua' or 'Joshua' means 'salvation', and only Jesus can give it (compare Acts 4:12). Think about how you could use this passage to explain to someone the deity of Christ.

Through the cross: Colossians 1:15–23

The cross of Jesus is the deepest enigma of our faith—God dying for man. Ask God to help you understand his great love as you probe these words. Why is Jesus given pre-eminence (18)? What difference does it make that nothing is outside his domain? What were we like that we needed to be reconciled to God (21)? How did the death of Jesus make our peace with God (20, 22; compare 2 Corinthians 5:21). What is God's ultimate purpose for us (22)?

Our holiness is so important to God that he sent Jesus to die that we might be made holy. How important is it to us?

By the grace of God: Titus 2:11–14

When Jesus appeared, so did the grace of God. That gift is free in the sense that there is no charge for it, but what it bids us to do after receiving the gift is costly. What action should we take now that God's grace has appeared? If God's *grace* appeared at Jesus first coming, his *glory* will be fully revealed at the second. Notice how Jesus' gift of himself has bought a people 'for himself'. Meditate for a few minutes on what it means to be owned by Jesus.

How is salvation applied to us?

We have been saved: John 5:24

This verse contains one of the greatest promises that could ever be made. In the context, Jesus is claiming the right to give life and to execute judgment. Now notice the conditions of the promise. If we believe God after hearing Jesus' claims to be doing God's works and speaking his words, what do we already have? What transition of status has already taken place? What do we no longer need to fear?

We are being saved: Philippians 2:12, 13

We know from other parts of the Bible that we cannot earn salvation. But according to this passage we do 'work it out'. Find another word in verse 12 which seems to be equivalent to working out one's salvation. Who is our model of obedience according to the context? How does God make it possible for us to obey him? The word for our outworking has the same root as that for God's in-working, and it is because he enables us to *want* to do right that we can do it. Take hold of God's promise and obey his command.

We will be saved: Hebrews 9:23–28

Jesus came once to put away sin. What is he doing now? Just as men die once, Jesus died only once. Why then is he coming a second time? Who will be saved when he returns? Now look back at the two passages above, and ask yourself what kind of person will be eagerly waiting for the return of Jesus.

7. Depression: a problem study

Realism Psalm 6

The first difficulty in studying what the Bible says on a problem is to locate the passages which deal with it. The best starting-point is to find a place where the problem is at least acknowledged, and then work outwards through related passages and issues. Here David expresses many of the symptoms of depression—fear, misery, bewilderment, tiredness, inadequacy, doubt. The Bible has no room for a happy-happy view which says no Christian should ever feel low. How did circumstances contribute to David's feeling? Who else in Scripture shares his experience?

Evil Ecclesiastes 3:16—4:8

The book of Ecclesiastes is a largely a cry of bewilderment at the ways of the world, which resolves itself in trust in God only at the very end. One of the most bewildering facts of life, especially for anyone who believes in God and his goodness, is the way bad people prosper so freely. In a way, the deeper our faith is, the bigger the problem becomes. What is your answer to it? What particular forms of wrong depressed the writer here? What are the modern equivalents? How do other biblical writers wrestle with the problem?

Persecution 2 Corinthians 1:8–10; 11:16–30

Much Christian depression arises from opposition. Jesus warned us of this so that we should not be alarmed by it (Mark 13:3–13; John 15:18—16:4). Paul is equally realistic about the problem and about the resources we have to meet it. What, in particular, bore upon Paul to make him 'utterly, unbearably crushed'? How far did the pressures come from (i) outside the church, (ii) inside the church, (iii) inside himself? What resources does he mention in 2 Corinthians with which to meet these challenges? (*Note:* the Greek word for 'comfort' in chapter 1 is related to Jesus' word for the Holy Spirit, the 'Comforter' or 'Counsellor', in John 14.)

Satan   Job 1

It is part of Christian realism to see the real, destructive personality behind so much of the evil in the world. What kind of activities are here attributed to Satan? This knowledge helps many of us (as it did Job) to come through depressing periods without blaming them on God. Jesus called the devil a murderer and a liar (John 8:44), and the New Testament also calls him the accuser of the brethren (Revelation 12:7–12). How might he use these roles to try to depress the Christian and make him ineffective? Where do guilt feelings come from?

Rest   1 Kings 19

Here is a classic expression of depression—'That's enough; take my life—I'm useless, I'm all alone' (4, 14)! Chapters 17 and 18 give the background to Elijah's feelings. Why did depression, rather than jubilation, follow such a great victory? What was the effect of fear—and what was the effect of sheer exhaustion? How did God restore the prophet's sense of proportion? Why did food and rest come before the voice of God? What is the place of rest, recreation, Sundays and holidays for today's Christian? Can one do too much praying, Bible study or 'Christian work'?

Guilt   Romans 5 : 12–21

Depression is often aggravated by guilt *feelings*, which have no real guilt behind them. These need to be resisted and removed; they have no claim upon us. Christians, however, believe that there is real guilt too, and this can only be removed by confessing it to God and receiving his forgiveness through Christ. We *ought* to be depressed until this happens, and elated when it does! What does this passage teach about real guilt and real freedom from it? What points of contrast does Paul draw between 'the trespass' and 'the free gift'? Read Romans 5–8 and Psalm 32.

Healing
John 5 : 1–24

What significance does the story attach to this man's (i) self-pity, (ii) faith, (iii) sin? Jesus speaks here of 'giving life'; what is included in that? Does it include freedom from depression? The story replies that some depression will not lift until we have been healed in a way that we cannot achieve by ourselves, and which may come from a variety of outside quarters. When would you send a depressed friend to (i) his doctor, (ii) a psychiatrist, (iii) his pastor, (iv) God? What kinds of healing can we expect directly from God today? In what terms would we pray with a depressed friend?

God
Romans 8 : 28–39

For all its realism at the practical level, the Bible never shrinks from saying that the deepest antidote to depression is religious—namely, an awareness of the reality of God and his love. Can you list five or more biblical characters for whom this was true? Have a look at Nehemiah 8:1–12. How many different lines of argument does Paul draw together to make his confident case in the Romans passage? This passage is often called 'unanswerable'; how might you try to answer it if you were writing anti-Christian propaganda to undermine people's confidence in their Christian faith?

Prayer
Philippians 4 : 1–20

If the reality of God undergirds our confidence, then intimate contact with him in prayer is bound to help. What specific result of prayer is here promised? How many different things are we told to do 'in the Lord'—and what does this mean? In what particular way might gloom be lifted by verse 8, 9 or 19? What is the secret of equilibrium which Paul says he has learned (12)? People often say they are depressed by the very difficulty of prayer itself; how would you help them? What other passages might be helpful?

Case study 1: Jacob Genesis 27–35

Take several bites at this longish study. If Jacob lived round the corner today we should probably say of him, 'He's had a hard life.' Devious parents, a dishonest employer, a tension-riddled marriage, fear of his brother, sordid and violent children—his life was a recipe for misery. (It continues in Joseph's story, pp. 84 ff.) How did these things in fact turn out to be experiences of growth and learning for him? His solutions were both profoundly spiritual and intensely practical: can you draw out the main features of his spiritual progress and the practical tips we might learn?

Case study 2: Asaph Psalm 77

Here is the problem of specifically religious depression: 'I believe in God; why isn't he wielding his power, fulfilling his promises and showing his love more obviously—especially to *me*?' As here, nostalgia is more the fruit of present melancholy than a precise recollection of earlier joy—and, as here, it distorts the things that are remembered, making them seem better than they really were. Only when the ·mood of 'especially me' begins to pass do the memories of God's work become more accurate and reassuring. The advice to 'count your blessings' need not be superficial. Asaph led in temple worship (1 Chronicles 16:5; 2 Chronicles 29:30); how does a leadership role complicate spiritual depression?

Case study 3: Peter and Jesus Luke 22 : 39–62

Here are two men in deep distress (44, 62)—one as he looks towards the future, the other from remorse at what he had done in the past. But 'we have not a high priest who is unable to sympathize with our weaknesses;' Jesus has been there before. The main battle was his temptation to evade the cross, though surely his dread was natural. Temptation, decision-making and facing the future can all make a valley; and failure in any of them can deepen it, as Peter found. How do you remedy the painful depression of failure, especially as a Christian?

Creativity   Exodus 31:1–11;
                               1 Kings 5:13—6:14; 8:54–66
Sorry for the unlikely readings, and their length! But these
two passages illustrate some of the truths in the creation
story (*e.g.* Genesis 1:28; 2:15): man is designed to be
creative, his skills come from God, and his creativity is highly
satisfying. This is why so much therapy includes painting or
gardening; such activities are healthy and recreative, and
they help if we get depressed. Why is the Bible so full of
architects' details? Are creative gifts limited to religious purposes? For what other purposes might God give them?
What do these sections say about humdrum work—and
how could Solomon's prayer apply to yours?

Fellowship   1 Corinthians 11:17–34
The church may seem depressing, but it should be the opposite—see the dynamic and supportive picture on pp. 81 ff.
and 106 ff. This particular group of Christians was failing in
three ways. (i) They were divided. How does the unity of a local
fellowship give strength to its members? (ii) They were incon-
siderate (how?). Can you see ways in which your own
fellowship is, too, and could be of more help to people who feel
'low'? (iii) It was scornful of the sacraments. What are these,
and how do they offer particular strength to a down-at-the-
mouth Christian?

Service   Philippians 1:1–18
This may sound like advertising, but Paul found Christian
work invigorating. Perhaps this is because it lifts our attention away from self-pity and on to Jesus Christ and the
needs of other people. What particular things brought Paul
joy, and how might we work towards them? At least four of
the factors we have already looked at are mentioned here;
can you spot them and say what Paul adds about them
here? What role does the Christian's hoped-for future have
in fighting his depression—and what does the New Testament say about that, here and elsewhere?

8. The Acts: grasping a big book

Many of the long historical sections of the Bible are worth reading rapidly the first time, before returning for detailed study later. The technique is to read two or three chapters for a broad view, then to focus on any verses of special significance. We now look at Acts in this way. Here Luke picks up the Jesus story at Jesus' own departure; he recounts the coming of the promised Spirit, the early growth of his people, and the opposition they aroused. Then follows the conversion of Saul, the opening of the message to non-Jews, and the rapid expansion of the church through Asia Minor and Greece to Rome itself.

The Spirit comes   1:10—2:47

These chapters record the obedience of the apostles, waiting in Jerusalem (no doubt uneasily) for Jesus' promise of power by his Spirit to be fulfilled; then the flowering of their faith and courage when he came. What is the significance of (i) Jesus' last words, (ii) the messengers' words, (iii) Peter's initiative in getting things organized before Pentecost? Focus on Peter's statement to the crowd (2:22–36); what are the main points, and what did they find so alarming about it? Should Christians today follow the example of having all their goods in common? If not, why not?

Power and persecution   3:1—4:31

Peter and John clearly continue to use the healing power of Christ for this man, and even the authorities cannot deny the fact. The pattern follows that of Jesus' own ministry; power, publicity, opposition. But what is noticeably different about this healing compared with those of Jesus himself? Focus on the dialogue with the authorities; what particular points did the apostles make to them? How far do their answers provide guidance for Christians under pressure today? They certainly believed in praying things over afterwards; can we learn from particular elements in their prayer?

Signs and wonders

4:32—5:42

The movement was clearly open to undermining from within as well as to assault from without. Focus this time on Ananias and Sapphira: what was their sin, actually? Why were they treated so severely? We are unlikely to make these particular mistakes, but what might be our equivalents? The Jewish leaders were 'filled with jealousy'—at what other times has that been a factor in Christian history? What did Peter mean about the Holy Spirit in 5:32? Gamaliel was a fine teacher and once had Paul among his students; but was he really so wise here?

Stephen

6:1—8:1a

It was not long before the sheer size of the work caused administrative problems. Was their principle of delegation sound, and if so, how might our churches better apply it? What were the qualifications looked for in the helpers? It seems that Stephen aroused criticism in the first place by comments along the same lines of his speech at his death; what was the main shape of his argument here? Why would the Jews find it so offensive? Signicantly, Saul makes his first appearance at this scene; what effect did it have upon him?

Christians at work

8:1b—9:31

The episode in Samaria presents a problem: why did Peter and John need to come down from Jerusalem? Were they alone capable of conveying the Spirit, or was there some blockage in Philip's message or in his hearers? Try some research to sort this out. More straightforwardly, there are three instructive interviews here. (i) Simon Magus and Peter: how far did Simon epitomize the Samaritan problem? Was Peter unduly hard on him? (ii) The Ethiopian and Philip: what might you learn from Philip's approach? (iii) Paul and Ananias: how far was Paul's influential future unlocked by this simple disciple's obedience?

Peter 9:32—11:18

God is clearly using Peter, as the Aeneas and Tabitha incidents show; yet he wants to go further and use him to initiate perhaps the biggest step yet. Why would the preparatory vision speak specially to a man like Peter? How was Peter's long-ingrained prejudice so quickly removed, and why was the role of the Holy Spirit so important? Do you learn anything from the conduct of the meeting in Jerusalem? Try putting together a pen-picture of Cornelius, who opened the door to this whole development. Does this fit any aspects of the ministry of Jesus himself?

Antioch to Antioch 11:19—13:52

The pace quickens, and you now need a map! In strategic Antioch in Syria, a group of quite ordinary Christians did spontaneously what Peter had done in Caesarea. Significantly, Barnabas and Paul provide a full follow-up teaching service (12:43); what does this say to us now? What does the episode with Herod Agrippa I and Peter teach about (i) prayer, (ii) miracles, (iii) common sense? Cyprus, Perga and Pisidian Antioch are just the beginning of Barnabas and Paul's extensive travelling work. What does the way they were chosen and commissioned say to our methods of Christian manpower deployment?

Problems all round 14:1—16:9

Can you begin to define the strategic principles by which Paul worked? Watch how they develop in his future work. The events in Lystra should be contrasted with John 20:24–29. In Acts 14:15–17, why did Paul and Barnabas begin with this part of their message in this situation? (Contrast Peter's approach in Acts 2:22–36). Why did they bother going back to Antioch to report? The issue in chapter 15 was fundamental to the spread of Christianity; what can we learn from the way they handled the dispute, and publicized their agreed decision (see chapter 16:4)? Given this decision, why did Paul circumcise Timothy?

Progress with setbacks 16:10—17:34

This passage begins one of the 'we-passages', which imply that Luke (the author) was with the party himself at these points. (These 'we-passages' are 16: 10–17; 20:5—21: 18; 27:1—28:16.) Why did Paul always go first to the known Jewish place of prayer, as in Philippi, or the synagogue, as in Thessalonica, Beroea and Athens? What distinguished his contact at Beroea from the others? Focus on Paul's speech at the Areopagus: what were the main lines of his argument when speaking to non-Jews, who would not share his assumptions? How far was the opposition they met (i) religious, (ii) political, (iii) commercial, (iv) cultural?

People and places 18:1—20:6

This colourful passage is full of individuals, and a mine of characters to study. Explore, for example, Silas, Gallio and Apollos (see, too, p. 126 ff.). It also calls for bringing the map up to date! Paul's treatment by the Jews and the Roman authorities in the various towns is worth comparing; it is more varied and complex than we often imagine. Chapter 19:1–7 can be confusing; it really underlines how well John had prepared for Jesus, but how radically different commitment to Jesus was, bringing as it did the essential hallmark of the Spirit.

Love and hate 20:7—22:1

Paul appears to have decided that he should keep the original church at Jerusalem informed of his activities (19:21), and then go on to Rome—though he could hardly have seen how it would happen. Focus here on Paul's address in Miletus: what do we learn from the example of his own work? Chapter 21 raises the question of how Christians are guided by God; was Paul right in disregarding the warnings he was sent? Were they to deter, or just to prepare him? What other factors were in his mind? Why did Paul agree to the rite of purification?

Defence and attack 22:2—23:35

Focus here on Paul's own account of his conversion and subsequent commissioning by the risen Jesus. What does it add to the account in chapter 9? Throughout this and the following sections, Paul makes much of his background—his Roman citizenship, his Jewish race and training, and his allegiance to the Pharisees. Does he do so legitimately? Was it devious to use his status to cause friction between the Romans and the Jews, the Sadducees and the Pharisees? What has God given you in background or status which could be deployed to his advantage?

Washing the hands 24:1—26:32

This story is reminiscent of the trial of Jesus in slow motion. Claudius Lysias smartly passes the buck to Felix, who procrastinates and leaves the problem to his successor; Festus does his best, but not without Agrippa's second opinion, and there is general relief when Paul can be despatched to Rome (where, in due course, the dithering begins again). How much of this is administrative, and how much were these men challenged personally by Paul's presence and teaching? Paul gives Agrippa a masterly combination of courtesy, doctrinal argument and personal testimony: how can we do that?

Rome unhindered 27:1—28:31

Paul's life is a fine example of God's providence at work. God delivered his servant out of danger into safety, and delivered him too into situations of usefulness. The scramble across the Mediterranean is a fitting last chapter but one! Paul on his side avoids flopping into his own concerns as we might, but takes every opportunity to present the Way, as they called it, to those he met. Can you list the openings he uses for teaching or evangelism en route? How far is Paul's closing statement (i) true, (ii) fair, (iii) a summary of Acts?

The use of the Old Testament in the New

The Old Testament was Jesus' Bible, and he held it in the highest respect; he regarded it as the medium of God's truth and the blueprint for his own mission. The New Testament writers have a similarly high view of it, quoting it around 300 times and alluding to it twice as often again. They always do so in a way that emphasizes its authority and divine origin, and we should let our view be shaped by theirs. The issue can be complex; here are some basic principles:

1 Ask why the author quoted the Old Testament passage. What would it mean to his readers?

2 The New Testament writers frequently quote from the Septuagint (Greek) version of the Old Testament. They may do so to make a play on words or because it came to mind most readily, or because the alternative was to make their own translation from the Hebrew (which they often did).

3 Sometimes New Testament authors are alluding to a passage with no intention of quoting it verbatim. Because they had no quotation marks or ellipsis marks, we cannot always tell exactly what was intended. They often paraphrased the text rather than quote it laboriously.

4 Sometimes New Testament writers are simply using biblical words in a way we would expect to find in anyone who was steeped in Scripture. Their words may be little more than reminiscent of a specific passage. This does not imply a loose attitude toward the words of the Bible but, on the contrary, shows that the words permeated the thinking of the New Testament writer so that they appear in his phrases.

5 The word 'fulfil' and its relatives are used in several different ways by New Testament authors. They may mean only that the present instance is similar to one in the Old Testament. Or they may mean that the Old Testament author was speaking specifically of this very historical event at hand. Or they may be saying one of several things in between.

9. Holiness: a word study

Sometimes it helps to study a single word or word group simply to get hold of one aspect of Christian truth. Holiness is an expansive and yet deep topic, because it deals with God's character and actions and our own—since we are called to imitate him. You do a word study by examining in context all the uses of a certain word and trying to put them together into a pattern. This section does some of the concordance work and categorizing for you. As you read each passage, keep asking, What does God want me to know about holiness? What should I do about it? Remember that different biblical writers may use the same words in slightly different ways. Take the references below at your own speed, and remember to read them in context.

What is the source of holiness?

Matthew 6:9	'Hallowed' means sanctified, holy.
1 Peter 1:14—16	What is the opposite of holiness? What reason is given for being holy?
Acts 4:27, 30	In what sense was Jesus holy?
Acts 2:27; 1:5	
Exodus 15:11	Moses' song asks a question which summarizes what the holiness of God means. There is no-one like him. Use this song to praise God for his holiness.

What is holiness?

Matthew 5—7	Christians are to be different.
Luke 2:23	The firstborn were set aside for, consecrated to, the Lord.
Acts 13:2, 3	'Set apart' = sanctify, make holy.
Ephesians 5:25—27	What is a holy church or person like?
1 Corinthians 6:9—11	Notice what holiness replaces.
2 Timothy 2:20—22	All of us want to be 'useful to the master'. Are you aiming at those qualities which will make you useful to the Lord Jesus?

How is holiness brought about?

John 17:17	How does 'the Word' sanctify us?
Romans 15:16; 2 Thessalonians 2:13; Romans 12:1, 2	Any sacrifice to God must be holy. How are we made acceptable for sacrifice?
1 Peter 1:2; 1 Corinthians 6:19, 20	What should be the result of sanctification by the Spirit?

What does holiness mean in practice?
An example

1 Thessalonians 4:1–8	Notice what sanctification means to God. It pleases him (1). It is his will (2). It is a reflection of the fact that we know God (5). Its alternative is the judgment of God (6). It is the purpose of the call of God (7). It is accomplished by the Holy Spirit of God (8). Think how verse 4 fits your definition of holiness.

How can we be 'sanctified' or 'saints', and still not be holy?

Acts 26:10; Romans 1:7; 8:27; 12:13; 16:2; 1 Corinthians 1:2; 2 Thessalonians 1; 10; etc.	God has called us to be holy and given us his holy name, his Holy Spirit, and his holy Word. By virtue of these gifts we are already different from the world. We have been set aside for God. The question is, do we live up to that calling and that new nature?

10. Joshua: God's leader

The book of Joshua is the first of the 'historical books' of Israel. This group of books includes the Prophets (Joshua, Judges, 1 and 2 Samuel, 1 and 2 Kings) and the Writings (1 and 2 Chronicles, Ezra and Nehemiah). It describes the entry and division of the promised land, after the people took forty years to complete a journey that could have been done in a matter of weeks. The point of all biblical history is that it reveals to us the character of God; it shows us what he is like and how he deals with his people. Because he has not changed, there are lessons in it for us to learn today. We must be careful, however, not to 'spiritualize' every aspect of what is a historical narrative. One of the important lessons to learn, and one which needs constant reiteration, is that these records *are* history and not fabrication. Having said that, though, don't miss the wealth of theological lessons to be grasped in this exciting book. Perhaps one of its major themes is that this side of heaven, all our 'arrivals' are but encouraging stage-posts on the journey. But more of that anon . . .

The commission
The God who promises   1 : 1–9

Joshua is not given a job for which he is unprepared (look up Exodus 17:8 ff.; 24:13; Numbers 14:6 ff. and Deuteronomy 34:9). Yet for all his natural ability and his God-moulded past, the immense task (2–4) is impossible without the continued presence and blessing of God (5). What is significant about the order of verses 5 and 6—first the promise, then the command? The stipulations are exacting (7, 8) and there is no glossing over them. Carefulness, however, does lead to prosperity. Why is the command to be of good courage not a vain one (9)?

Entering the land

Mobilization 1 : 10–18

Many scholars place the entry and conquest in the thirteenth century BC. There are two striking features in this account. (i) This army is clearly organized and disciplined (10, 11) compared with the rabble which left Egypt. The spiritual lessons learnt in the wilderness have had very practical results. (ii) There is not only discipline but there is also unity (12–18). Any enterprise undertaken by the people of God, and especially one of this magnitude, requires practical allegiance to one another. There is no place for words only (14, 16, 17) and disobedience will be met with more than words (18).

Reconnaissance 2 : 1–24

The land is to be taken by campaigns in the centre, the south, and the north. Jericho is the key to it all (1), and trust in God's promises does not preclude spying out the land; rather, it demands such activity (2–7). Rahab is commended in the New Testament (Hebrews 11:31), not for her immorality or her falsehood, but for her faith in God. It is not just because she is frightened, but because the evidence has convinced her that the true God fights for Israel (8–10). What do we learn from the way the men dealt with her (14–20)?

Knowing where to go 3 : 1–13

This dramatic episode reminds the people that they are about to embark on a holy war—the ark is a symbol of God's presence and contains the tablets of the Ten Commandments (3; Exodus 25:12) and the fact that they have to consecrate themselves is vivid testimony to the nature of the war (5). God always leads the way (6) and gives his leaders the necessary authority (7). Unlike many modern 'prophets' and leaders, whose pronouncements are sometimes so vague as to be useless, or which quite simply do not come true, Joshua's words are precise and accurate (10, 13). See *The New Bible Commentary Revised* for a fascinating insight into verse 4.

The memorable crossing   3:14—4:10a

Interesting parallels have occurred since this famous blockage
(15–17)—notably as a result of an earthquake in 1927—but a
natural explanation in no way detracts from the miraculous
timing of the event. Just as their exit from Egypt was fixed in
their minds by peculiar circumstances, so their entry into Ca-
naan impressed itself on 'the national memory'.* It is worth
studying the cairns of the Old Testament; none are without
significance and all are there for children and adults alike (6).
God does give his people fixed points as reminders. What are
yours?

A God worth fearing   4:10b–24

A God of our own invention, whom we could manipulate,
would need to fear us, not vice versa. This story is of a God who
is ahead of us as well as behind us. The climax of the account is
the reason given to explain the events (24). The God of Israel is
not play-acting. He has real power, and it's not only his own
people who need to fear him, but all the peoples of the earth
(24). His human agent should be feared too (14). What does it
mean for a New Testament Christian to 'fear God'?

The indelible mark   5:1–15

Circumcision was the rite God gave to identify his people
(Genesis 17:9–14). What is the Christian equivalent
(Colossians 2:11, 12)? Circumcision is personal and indelible,
and it speaks of a restored relationship. In the wilderness they
had been under the judgment of God (6; Numbers 14:34) and
had presumably been taunted by the Egyptians during their
wandering (9). No uncircumcised male could eat the Passover
(Exodus 12:43–49). What does the Passover commemorate
and why is this a significant time for its reintroduction? Note
that God doesn't waste time giving us things we don't need
(12).

*F. F. Bruce, *Israel and the nations* (Paternoster Press, 1973), p. 17.

Obeying the rules 6:1–14

Children love this episode, but what are we adults to make of it? It is in the Bible for better reasons than merely providing dramatic material for harassed Sunday-school teachers! The precise instructions (3–5), the regularity and persistence of the exercise (9–14) and the absence of immediate results (3) are all things worth pondering. There are many more features like this. How many can you find, and how do they apply today? The trumpets were ceremonial ones; it was a religious exercise, not a military one. Note the difference in the position of the ark (compare 3:4 and 6:9)—what does it signify?

A necessary destruction 6:15–27

It all seems a bit drastic and severe, but the story stands in all its stark reality. It is not there by mistake, so what are we to learn from it? Try and work it out for yourself before you read the next sentence! The destruction is testimony to the depths of depravity to which Jericho had sunk, and it is a reminder that God cannot but take sin seriously. How does obedience safeguard Israel's purity (18) and what truths does Rahab exemplify (Hebrews 11:13; James 2:25)?

Doing what you are told 7:1–26

God is not to be trifled with. His commands cannot be lightly set aside (1), nor can his stipulations be quietly ignored (11, 12). He cannot be deceived (16–23), nor can his anger be appeased without drastic and serious action (13–15). The awful truth of this passage is that individual offences have corporate consequences (7–9, 11, 15), which deeply affect the life and destiny of the nation. Can you think of New Testament teaching to the same effect? What is the appropriate Christian response to sin within the church (25)? Secret sin is no secret to God.

A victory for strategy

8 : 1–29

Having put things right (7:25, 26), fear and dismay are un-necessary and further action possible (1). The account has many tell-tale marks of shrewdness— *e.g.* taking all the fighting men (1) was good for morale, even if they were not all needed—and the military deception is amongst the classics of history. The fact of having the Lord on your side does not mean that you need not use your loaf! Ai remains an archeological puzzle, and verse 28 is still true today. The victory, however, was certainly an important one, for it opened up the whole cen-tre of the country.

The God who makes conditions

8 : 30–35

This is a holy war.* It is not only that God's presence sanctifies it, but his word demands it. Not only is there a physical fight (1–29), but a moral one too (30–32). This people's religion is central, not peripheral, and so this ceremony of covenant renewal is of paramount importance. At the heart of it all is the morality of God (31, 32) and so there is nothing that you can overlook or leave out, nor anybody to whom it does not apply (35). Look up Deuteronomy 11:26–32 and 27:1–26. They are solemn things to which to say 'Amen'.

The southern campaign

A crafty move

9 : 1–27

God's people live in the real world and are not automatically protected from trickery; deception is part of the opposition's strategy, and it was Jesus who beautifully described how we should react (Matthew 10:16). What feature of the Israelites' action made it compromise and disobedience (25), and what was their basic mistake (14)? Having discovered the decep-tion, however, they remain true to their word (18) and they spare the Gibeonites' lives for service (19–21). In all this it is clear that God is sovereign (27) and in fact the deception opens up a further part of the land.

* On moral questions raised by the holy-war ideal see J. W. Wenham, *The goodness of God* (Inter-Varsity Press, 1974), chapter 8.

Honouring contracts   10:1–15

The people of Israel serve a God who is true to his word, and so they must be the same (6, 9:15). It would have been easy to argue themselves out of their commitment—the opposition was strong and united (1–5) and their contract was disobediently and foolishly made. The promise had been made, however, and the Lord's assurance given (8), so the action was swift and ambitious (9, 10). God uses people who get on with the job, but he does not always confirm their work by such extraordinary interventions (11–14). What do you make of verse 14?

Remarkable victories   10:16–42

This is a very impressive catalogue of military successes, covering a large area (40–43, look it up in a Bible atlas) and capturing and executing the powerful kings (18, 23, 26). If you get a chance to visit some of these sites, it will for ever remain imprinted on your memory just how remarkable these victories were. The success was indeed miraculous (42) for these sites were very strongly fortified and to take each one was a major operation. Lachish, Eglon and Debir each show signs of violent and complete destruction about this time (1250–1200 BC). Note the place to which they returned (43; 5:9, 10).

The northern campaign

A bloody business   11:1–23

Joshua's success in the south stimulated the formation of a huge army of allies in the north. To get a good picture of it all, you need to do your homework on the geography and the life-style of the period. Hazor was a very big city covering almost 200 acres and with about 40,000 inhabitants. The site was excavated during the 1950s and 60s, and the evidence points to such a destruction and indicates that the city was full of temples for sun-god worship. Why is the defeat of the Anakim specifically mentioned (Numbers 13:33)?

The conquered kings   12 : 1–24

It is very interesting to see how people approach a chapter such
as this. For many it is a list of strange names which mean
nothing and whose recital merely hardens the feeling of
irrelevance. Others, though—perhaps those of a more imaginative frame of mind—are able to enter into the momentous nature of this incredible military success. We live in an age
when most of the imaginative hard work is done for us by the
television producers and their research teams. Perhaps it is
time we did our own research. What does the chapter tell us
about God?

Dividing the land

Still a lot to do   13 : 1–14

The allocation of the land is a complicated business
(13:1–19:51) and it is worth getting a broad outline in your
mind before having a detailed look. (*The New Bible Commentary Revised* is especially helpful; see p. 247.) It is clear that a
complete subjection of the land had not yet been achieved (1),
that large areas were still occupied by the original inhabitants,
and that the Lord was going to work (6) through individual
tribes in their allotted areas (7). Only the Levites were to have
no tribal area—an instruction left by Moses (Numbers
18:20–24; 35:1–8). Draw some spiritual lessons for your own
life and that of your local church.

Coming into an inheritance   13 : 15–33

It is always a great moment when you finally receive what you
have been promised some time before. Coming into an inheritance is a time for paying attention to details; you don't
want to miss out on anything! Imagine the emotion of first sur-
veying and then entering this precious land which you had been
promised years before and for which you had led a nomadic
existence for the past forty years. As Christians, what is our inheritance, and are we as excited about the details as our
forefathers were?

The rewards of faithful service 14:1-15

What an attractive person Caleb was. It is hardly even a sketch that these verses draw, and yet we instinctively see what sort of man he was—a brave man, to spy out the land (compare Deuteronomy 1:22–36); a man prepared to be different and come to opposite conclusions from the majority (compare Numbers 14:20–30); and a humble man, aware of the Lord's sovereignty (10, 12). How good it is to find someone not content to rest on his laurels (11, 12)! When the people of God are weak-kneed, someone with a different spirit is required (Numbers 14:24).

Getting the boundary right 15:1-12

There were two especially powerful sections of the nation, Judah and Joseph (the latter comprising the two half-tribes of Ephraim and Manasseh). The land given to Judah was large, fertile in the north and more desert-like in the south. Boundaries are always important, the subject of many a debate and argument. Nations still go to war against one another over them. Exact maps are crucial, and this detailed account betrays the meticulous nature of the Giver of the land. His moral boundaries are no less rigorously defined, and vague delineation leads only to trouble. What spiritual counterpart may the 'natural' features of the land have?

Placing the families 15:13-63

The man who knows what it is to be rewarded has learnt how to give generously in his turn (16, 17). His generosity is lavish too (18, 19). Jesus had some pertinent remarks on this subject. Can you remember what they were (Luke 12:48)? Can you remember some Old and New Testament situations where God gave generously but the recipients forgot to act in the same way? Not a few of the listed cities have changed their names (20–63), though some remain the same today. Clearly society was based around the family structure within each tribe, and this structure was given geographical identity.

Compromise 16 : 1–10

The process of allotment continues and Manasseh and Ephraim receive their inheritance (4). Ephraim is a proud and stubborn tribe (a theme worth tracing through Judges) and it may be significant that the verb for their refusal to drive out the Canaanites is 'did not' (19) in contrast to Judah (15:63) and Manasseh (17:12) where it is 'could not'. Wilful compromise is an offence to God, and its consequences are unavoidable. Gezer did not become an Israelite city until the time of Solomon (1 Kings 9:16, 17). Instructions are to be obeyed, not dodged.

A shrewd decision 17 : 1–18

A case could be made out for saying that Israel was a male-orientated society, and yet specific provisions for women were inbuilt (3–6). The daughters of Zelophehad claimed the possession in line with Moses' stipulations for families without sons (Numbers 27:1–11; 36:1–12). The promise of wisdom and courage made to Joshua on entering the land (chapter 1) was not only for the conquest but for the subsequent settlement as well. His dealing with the tribe of Joseph (14–18) is characteristically shrewd. What lessons can we learn here in dealing with awkwardness and pride in God's people?

Getting on with the job 18 : 1–28

Shiloh was the first Hebrew sanctuary to be set up. The tabernacle was housed there and it was the focus for Israel's worship. The site can be visited today, and its barrenness fits its history well (look up 1 Samuel 1:3, 4:4, 10, 11, 22; Jeremiah 7:12 and Psalm 78:56–62). God is not dilatory, and his people should not be so either (3). In fact, there is one thing about which God is slow: what (Nehemiah 9:17)? The work needed to be done painstakingly (8, 9), a good record made (9), and the allotment process carried out 'before the Lord' (10).

The work continues   19:1–51

The details may seem tedious to us, but each city with its surrounding villages is specifically designated and the title deeds
given to each tribe. This gave both security and responsibility—security, for the record was signed and sealed;
responsibility, for if the inhabitants were unsubdued it was that
particular tribe's fault. Simeon's inheritance was next door to
Judah's belligerent western neighbours and was a fulfilment of
Genesis 49:5–7. Dan's inheritance seems to have been too
small, and also Judah failed to hold the coastal plain. The site
where this distributing process took place is again mentioned
(51), so that no-one could doubt the identity of the Distributor.

Necessary refuges   20:1–9

The provision of six cities of refuge was made by Moses—three
to the east and three to the west of Jordan (Numbers 35:9–34;
Deuteronomy 19:1–10) and the particular cities they chose
are strategically placed (7, 8). They were to act as regulative
devices, to combat hasty and misguided revenge. They
provided a fair trial for the accused, who, if proved guilty, would
be handed over to the 'avenger of blood'. But if he was innocent, he would be specially protected for a definite time (6). For
a fascinating and illuminating account of Old Testament
morality read Derek Kidner's *Hard sayings* (IVP, 1972).

The one who does not fail   21:1–45

The Levitical cities had been promised by Moses (Numbers
35:1–8) along with pasture land. Clearly the cities were not in-
habited exclusively by Levites, but they were given a special
place in each city; for their function as custodians of the
nation's spiritual life did not preclude provision for their basic
necessities (18:7). They were thus diffused throughout the nation (41). The concluding verses (43–45) are a beautiful climax
to the preceding chapters, for though the latter seem to have
been dominated by human activity, they really describe the
grace of God, for both the land (43) and the rest (44) are the gift
of God.

A misunderstanding cleared up 22 : 1–34

The two and a half tribes had faithfully completed their obligations and Joshua gives them a charge (4, 5) and a blessing (6). On the western bank of the Jordan (10) they build a great altar, the purpose of which is completely misunderstood by the remaining tribes (11, 12), who send a powerful delegation (see Numbers 25 : 6–8) to size up the situation in the light of Leviticus 17 : 8, 9. They had their history and theology lessons right (17–20)! They were satisfied with the account offered (21–34)—indeed their attitude towards the departing tribes (11) substantiated the latter's fears of isolation.

Past and future

The key to success 23 : 1–16

There has been astonishing success in the conquest and occupation of a well-fortified land by a nomadic people. There is no explanation other than verse 3, no guarantee for the future other than verses 6–8 and no recipe for failure other than verses 12–13. The striking thing about the preceding chapters (18–22) is that the people are already failing—to obey the law (6), to remain separate (7, 12), to remain loyal (8) and to love God supremely (11). The arrival in the promised land has not made them perfect: does this fact have a New Testament parallel? (Also, refer back to the Joshua introduction.)

The need to choose 24 : 1–33

Joshua's final address emphasizes two necessities—first for evidence and secondly for a verdict. Israel's God is for real; he is powerful, loving and generous (2–13). Because he is for real, a definite choice has to be made (14, 15) and no merely vague adherence can be entertained (19–24). All of us are tempted to deal falsely with God (27). He cannot do so with us; he can neither excuse our rebellion (19, 20) nor fail to acknowledge faithful service (29). The devastating thrust of verse 15 is that *if* you are not going to serve God, then choose any god you like; they are all equally impotent.

Using a concordance

A concordance is a book which lists the occurrences of particular words in the Bible so that we can see what the Bible says on that subject. Its name comes from the Latin word for harmony and thus implies that the Bible speaks harmoniously.

For most of us the best thing to use is an *analytical concordance* which lists the English words alphabetically but then shows which Greek or Hebrew words it is translating; in this way we can get behind the translation to the original without needing to know Greek and Hebrew. This helps because often one English word translates two or more different ones in the original, as when *love* translates both *agapē* and *philia*. A concordance can be big and expensive and it may be worth having a cheap paperback one while you are saving up; try to buy one which is based on the version you normally read, study and memorize. Use your concordance:

1 to see the Bible's whole teaching on a subject
2 to find half-forgotten passages when you know at least one prominent word
3 to discover more fully how the biblical writers use a word; one word may have different connotations.
4 to underscore the importance of a doctrine by seeing how often a word is used (*e.g.* 'faith' occurs more than 200 times in the New Testament)
5 to balance conclusions drawn from single passages by comparing them with other references (*e.g.* when all the references to 'harden' or 'hardness of heart' are studied in context one sees that God is not capriciously making people incapable of responding to him as some passages might seem to imply (Exodus 4:21, Romans 9:18). Rather, he is allowing disobedience and rebellion to have its expected effect.)

Caution: The great danger in using a concordance is that we fail to read the passages in their entirety or in context. Avoid this pitfall, and the concordance can be a great help in growing in the knowledge of God's Word.

11. Portrait gallery: some New Testament characters

Using character studies

Studying individual characters in the Bible helps us to put flesh on distant events and see how God's message applied in real human experience. Sometimes two stories run parallel, but even then we gain two points of view on a single set of events (*e.g.* from Peter and John writing about Christ, or Jeremiah and Ezekiel prophesying about the exile). A good concordance (see p. 125) will help you track down all the passages where an individual is mentioned. Explore the context and work out a careful chronology; then you can build up the story through the person's words, actions and relationships.

Bartimaeus
Mark 10 : 46–52

No end of helpful character studies grow from looking at Jesus' own meetings with people. This particular story is full of double meanings; how far was Bartimaeus really blind? How did his view of Jesus compare with that of the crowd? Or with that which Jesus had himself been explaining in the previous verses? Do you attach any significance to the place where Bartimaeus lived, his place in society, or his 'following Jesus on the way'? Is it legitimate to see him as a picture of those who call upon Christ today—and if so, what do we learn?

Judas
Here is a sad story full of difficult questions. (Find the passages for yourself—there could be about fifteen.) Judas was probably the only Judean among the twelve disciples, the others being from Galilee. Is this why he stuck out? Why did Jesus choose him—and how much do you think Jesus knew at the time? What turned Judas off—the money; the demands of Jesus; disappointed political ambitions?

How was he influenced by Jesus, the other disciples, the chief priests, and Satan? If Satan entered into him, how is he to blame?

Barnabas and Saul

Sometimes light is shed by looking at a person from two sides of a relationship. Barnabas played a key role in winning acceptance for Saul of Tarsus as a Christian leader, but was then overtaken by him in influence and intellectual power. For this study, find the references to Barnabas in the Acts of the Apostles and watch this developing relationship. Can you highlight six vital points at which Barnabas contributes to the story? Where do Barnabas and Saul begin to be referred to as Paul and Barnabas? How did Barnabas cope with the shift in importance?

Paul and Barnabas

Look over the story in Acts from Paul's point of view; then dig out the references to Barnabas in Galatians, Colossians and 1 Corinthians. What do the contexts of these remarks tell us about Barnabas and his attitude to the issues involved? (It will help to read the whole of Galatians to follow some of this.) Why did the issues matter? How important was it for the leaders to agree over them? Why was Paul willing to disagree so sharply—and at what points? What was the aftermath of their disagreements?

Epaphroditus

This is an easy one! You may therefore like to give the time to reading through Philippians to set him in context. What kind of atmosphere did he come from and what kind of relationship did Paul have with the Philippian Christians? Find and read the passages in Acts which recount the gospel's arrival there. Paul's five titles for Epaphroditus build an impressive picture; what does each title tell you? Paul reserves these compliments for only a handful of his colleagues; can you track down which of these are used for whom?

Lydia

It's high time to include a woman—especially while the Philippian background is in your mind. What was Lydia's particular contribution, and where in Philippians might Paul be referring to her? She came from Thyatira and may well have helped in building a Christian church there; where is this church spoken of in the New Testament—and what is said? Think about some of the Bible's other women; were their gifts and contributions as stereotyped as the churches often make them appear today? How does Christianity view women differently from the common view, then and now?

Aquila and Priscilla

A little research ought to put this couple's life into four episodes—Rome to Corinth, Corinth to Ephesus, Ephesus to Rome, Rome to Ephesus. The edict of Claudius mentioned in Acts 18:2 is recorded by the Roman historian Suetonius, who says that in AD 49 the emperor expelled the Jews from Rome because of rioting 'on account of one Chrestus' (Christ); the gospel had arrived! Using background books as well as the text, can you sort out (i) what was remarkable about their marriage in the first place, (ii) how they used their home, (iii) the future career of Apollos?

Onesimus

Onesimus was Philemon's slave. Where did he live, and how does this story fit into the rest of the New Testament? Onesimus's name means 'useful' or 'beneficial'—hence Paul's play on these words and ideas in his letter to Philemon. How does Paul's letter challenge accepted attitudes to slavery in his day—and how does it challenge modern attitudes to it? This same Onesimus may well have become the later bishop of Ephesus by that name, and possibly also the first collector of Paul's letters. What could that fact say to the modern church?

128

Timothy, learner

For this study, try to pick up Timothy's story in Acts and the scattered references in Paul's letters (except 1 and 2 Timothy). This should give an idea of how his movements fit into Paul's, and how Paul trained him as a Christian leader of the future. How did he do this in particular (i) by his own friendship and company, (ii) by sending him on assignments with other trusted colleagues, (iii) by giving him spheres of responsibility of his own? Paul was utterly opposed to those Jewish Christians who still insisted on circumcision (see Galatians 2); why then did he circumcise Timothy?

Timothy, teacher

For this look at Paul's letters to Timothy (focusing on the first, as we study the second in more depth in section IV). Timothy always comes across as young, timid, and unsure of himself. From these two studies, can you see the stresses which made him like that and the steps Paul took to help him?

From 1 and 2 Timothy, how would you list the qualities needed in a future Christian leader, and the priorities such a leader should adopt? What are the dangers mentioned and advice given (i) at the doctrinal level, and (ii) at the practical level?

Further character studies

The studies above are only a tiny sample. Other suggestions might include (from the Gospels) Jesus' mother, his aunt Elizabeth, and his cousin John the Baptist; Peter, James, John and Thomas among the twelve; Legion, Zacchaeus, Nicodemus; and Martha, Mary and Lazarus. From elsewhere: Titus, Dorcas, Silas, Luke, John Mark, Tychicus, Aristarchus, Epaphras, Apollos, Stephen and Philip; or (on the darker side) Demas, Ananias and Sapphira, Simon Magus and Elymas. Then of course there is the whole of the Old Testament, running from full-scale portraits of Abraham, Moses, David or Isaiah, to the cameos of Abraham's servant, Gideon, Ruth, Esther and Jonah.

12. Evangelism: a topical study

The model
Matthew 4:19

This verse is worth memorizing, and like all others it should be studied in context. Early in Jesus' ministry, he makes it plain that others are to share his task of calling people to repent—to turn from sin to God. What does Jesus demand of the fishermen? Why must following Jesus come first? What does Jesus promise to do for them? It's not good enough to follow the parts of Jesus' life-style which are easy or appealing. We must also follow his lead as he fearlessly proclaims, 'Repent, for the kingdom of heaven is at hand.'

Our motives and message
2 Corinthians 5:11–21

Paul says 'We persuade men' (11) and 'we beseech you' (20). The question is, Why? What is to be our attitude toward those with whom we talk (13–15)? Of what central facts of the gospel must we be convinced (14–19)? Where do we get our message (18)? It would be arrogant to go out proclaiming a home-made message. Our message comes from God, and we represent him, not the church. But notice how far the passage goes beyond that (20). Look at Luke 10:16 for a sobering implication of this truth.

Keeping yourself in perspective
2 Corinthians 4:1–11

Sharing the faith can all too easily become talking about oneself or twisting the Bible to avoid a clash with someone else's ideas. What pitfalls are we to avoid? Why will some people reject our gospel (3, 4)? Openly speaking the truth will take away other obstacles of conscience, but that doesn't mean we rely on our own power or goodness. In fact, how does God use our weakness (7)? It is when we are identified with Jesus *in his death* that people see the life of Jesus and accept it.

Our attitude toward evangelism Romans 1 : 14–16
If someone is going to proclaim a message enthusiastically
he must believe in it passionately. Notice that Paul believed
that the gospel is universal. It is not solely for religious people or those from a Christian background, or for the poorly
educated or unsophisticated. What *is* the gospel (16)? That
powerful conviction focuses our attention on a needy world
for whom the message we spread can mean salvation. How
does that knowledge affect Paul's attitude towards the
gospel? However foolish it may seem, if it releases the
saving power of God we need not be ashamed, but, like
Paul, should be eager to preach the good news.

Readiness for unexpected opportunities
1 Peter 3 : 13–17
For most early Christians, Christian living (which includes
proclaiming the gospel) meant suffering. Notice what forms
it took. In such cases of suffering for righteousness, what is
to be our reaction (i) to Jesus, (ii) in terms of our own
behaviour, (iii) when we get a chance to speak for Christ?
How we speak is as important as what we say. Are you
living in such a way that anyone would persecute you for
righteousness and ask you to tell them why you have such
hope? What would you say if you had to answer right now?
Are you prepared?

God's priority   Luke 15 : 1–32
Jesus was being criticized for associating with known
sinners. These three familiar parables explain his behaviour
in terms of what God thinks is important. Notice verses 7,
10 and 32. Let your mind get hold of the fact that God and
all heaven rejoice when someone who was lost is found.
What a privilege to be able to give joy to God! The searching
question is, how do we reach the 'lost' if we associate only
with the 'found'? Ask God to give you meaningful friendships
with unbelievers. Like Jesus, may we be willing to 'receive
sinners and eat with them'.

IV
Meat:

a way in to
more solid study

Don't be put off! 'Solid food is for the mature' (according to Hebrews 5:14). We're not aiming to make your study dull, but to give increasing satisfaction to the appetite of a growing Christian. You will be wanting more substantial food, and more of it; and this section aims to help you get it! We are trying to go a little further behind the scenes of Scripture, to tackle some of the more difficult passages, and to look at some of the issues you might not have met in the early days of Christian life. But we are also trying to leave you on your own a bit so that you are increasingly able to study for yourself without our assistance. So if there are times when you feel we are not giving you as much help as we might, that is quite deliberate.

1. Romans: a book to grapple with

Coleridge called the Epistle to the Romans 'the most profound writing extant'. Many Christians through the centuries would echo that sentiment. The statement shouldn't frighten us away from a serious study of the book, but it should remind us that we will be only scratching the surface of its riches.

Paul wrote this letter from Corinth while on his way to Jerusalem with a gift for the saints there. He wrote it to inform the Roman Christians of his intention to visit them, and also to give them a logical and thorough presentation of the gospel. Maybe he felt this was necessary because he had not personally visited them, even though they were certainly part of his flock since he was the apostle to the Gentiles.

First read the three sections (in three sittings if possible):

1 Salvation (chapters 1–8)
2 The history of salvation (chapters 9–11)
3 The salvation life (chapters 12–15:13)

Next, study the book by reading the passage given, but concentrating on the verses in brackets. For instance, on the first day of study read 1:1–7, but concentrate on verses 1, 6 and 7. On the second day, read 1:1–17, but concentrate on verses 1–6. This plan of overlapping readings should help you grasp the whole as well as parts of the letter. The following outline, based on Godet's commentary, may give you a clearer idea of where the argument is going:

1:1–15	Preamble. Paul's apostleship, the subject of the gospel, Paul's plans
1:16–17	The gospel in a nutshell
1:18—5:21	
1:18—3:28	The lostness of man
3:21—5:11	Justification by faith, based on the work of Christ
5:12–21	Contrasting the first and the second Adam
6:1—8:39	Participating in the life of Christ
9:1—11:36	How can God reject the chosen people?
12:1—15:13	Practical outworking of the gift of salvation
15:14—16:27	Concluding remarks and instructions

The brief notes are not intended to exhaust the passages. Keep studying, praying and thinking. Make your own observations, conclusions and applications.

Paul, the author   1 : 1–7 (1, 6, 7)
Notice how Paul designates himself. It is because he was willing to be a servant of Christ that God called him to be an apostle. God was at work in Paul's life from before the beginning (Galatians 1:15). Even though we will not have Paul's authoritative position, all Christians have the relationship with Jesus which he describes. What do the other synonyms for a Christian imply (6, 7)?

The gospel concerns Jesus   1 : 1–17 (1–6)
Paul introduces himself as 'set apart for' the gospel. Where does the gospel come from? Who is its subject? Notice that the description of Jesus in verse 4 does not mean that he became God's Son at the resurrection. That would contradict Romans 8:3 and many other passages. The idea is more that Jesus was restored to the full glory and power of his nature by the resurrection. Faith and obedience are inextricably linked: obedience to truth demands faith; faith produces obedience. From verse 5, work out a missionary mandate: think about the basis, call, power, and goal of mission.

The priority of prayer   1 : 8–15 (8–10, 13)
How would you describe Paul's prayer for the Roman Christians? What does it spring from (5, 6, 9)? How do human intuitions (13) fit together with prayer? How did Paul respond to the frustration of unanswered prayer (9)? What would God say about your prayers?

Purposeful visiting   1 : 8–15 (11–13)
Look for a twofold purpose for Paul's visit to Rome, one concerning Christians, the other concerning outsiders. Note that fruit-harvesting 'among you' may mean evangelism in Rome, but

may also mean helping Christians develop the fruit which we are to bear (John 15:8). How does our common faith lead to mutual encouragement? Re-examine your contact with other Christians. Are you using your gifts to build them up? Are you similarly allowing them to encourage you?

Divine indebtedness   1 : 8–15 (14–15)
This passage speaks of the 'ought' of preaching the gospel. This sense of obligation came from Christ (1:5) and leads to an eagerness to preach the gospel. Below are some passages which use the same Greek word as Paul does here. As you read them, let God grip you with a godly sense of obligation to those who have not heard the gospel.

Matthew 18:28; 23:16, 18 (bound); Luke 11:4; 13:4 (offenders), 17:10 (duty); John 13:14; Romans 8:12; 15:1; 1 Corinthians 7:3; 9:10; 2 Corinthians 12:14; Ephesians 5:28; 2 Thessalonians 1:3; 1 John 2:6; 3:16; 4:11.

We owe it to the world to preach the gospel.

Is God hiding?   1 : 18–32 (18–23)
Examine this passage closely to see what Paul is saying about individual responsibility. What has God done? What would you say to someone who protested that he did not believe in God, as if that would end the conversation? Suppressing *the* truth renders people less sensitive to truth generally. How does that work out in practice?

The wrath of God made plain   1 : 18–32 (24–32)
Notice that the wrath of God against his enemies consists not so much in oppression as in allowing them to reap what they have sown. What conclusions can one draw about homosexuality from this passage? Notice the other 'more acceptable sins' mentioned alongside it. Those who refuse to honour God soon dishonour themselves. Notice verse 32. It is one thing to have a 'besetting sin' which grieves you into repentance and confession. All Christians share that experience to some degree. It is quite another matter to adjust your values to fit practices which you know to be evil.

What's wrong with judging? 2 : 1–29 (1–11)

Paul wants to make it clear that Jewishness is no special protection against God's wrath unless it is accompanied by obedience. Why had God not already judged the Jews? What are we acknowledging when we judge someone else? What is the basis of God's judgment? What do the two groups of people have to look forward to?

The inadequacy of the law 2 : 1–29 (12–29)

The law cannot give life; it can only tell us when we fall short. Hearing the law is not enough; obeying it is essential. What might be the consequences *for others* if we break God's law (24)? Although verse 29 is speaking of Judaism, it contains an important insight into true Christianity. No matter how acceptable we may appear to other people, God is the one whose praise we must have.

Man's predicament 3 : 1–26 (1–20)

Paul's imaginary Jewish opponents ask two further questions (1, 9). What are the advantages of being a Jew if the law doesn't bring justification? If the law serves only to condemn, why aren't those without it in a better position (9–18)? Everyone sins. Try to write a helpful definition of sin from verses 10–18. What areas of our lives does it touch? Why will every mouth be stopped before God? Notice that verse 20 puts us all on exactly the same footing before God.

The factual basis of justification 3 : 9–26 (21–26)

Paul labours the point that the work of Christ manifested the righteousness of God (21, 22, 25, 26). Nothing less than God's character is at stake. How does the death of Jesus preserve God's righteousness? Notice who took the initiative (25). What is required of those who want to receive God's gift (22, 25, 26)? Look up the technical words in a Bible dictionary, concordance or commentary.

So what? 3 : 21–31 (27–31)

The beautiful doctrine that everyone is justified by faith was not meant for speculative contemplation. What does it imply about boasting? about the law? about God's jurisdiction? Think about this passage until you can see clearly some of the present-day implications of justification by faith.

A test case: Abraham   4:1–25 (1–5, 9–12)
If anyone could boast, Abraham could—at least by human standards. How was he made righteous *in God's sight?* When verse 5 speaks of 'one who does not work', what does it mean?

What conclusion does Paul draw from the fact that Abraham was circumcised *after* he was declared righteous? What earlier verse in Romans does this passage re-emphasize?

A test case: David   4:1–25 (6–8)
If Abraham is remembered for his works which came from faith, David is often recalled as one whose sins were painfully conspicuous. Read all of Psalm 32 and take hold of its promises.

Real children of Abraham   4:1–25 (13–25)
God's promise was to Abraham and his descendants (Genesis 12:1–3; 17:4–8). The question Paul answers here is, Who are Abraham's real children? On what does the promise rest? What kind of God did Abraham believe in (17)? Notice that Abraham did not simply believe in a supernatural God—he believed in a God who could and would keep his promises, however impossible it seemed. What should our faith be like? What evidence for God's nature do we have which Abraham did not have?

The blessings of justification   5:1–14 (1–11)
God's gift of justification is one large package with many presents inside. Study these verses until you understand what the presents are and how they are related to each other. We are to love others as God loved us. Think about how and when God showed his love for us (6, 8, 10). If God gave his costliest gift to his enemies, what can we expect now that we are his beloved children? Why do we rejoice in any circumstances?

The first Adam   5:12–21
In Hebrew, Adam means mankind. So the first man was both a real individual and the head of a whole race. His disobedience

138

had certain effects on all his descendants—even those who lived before Moses. What are they? What is God's response to sinful behaviour (16)? Death still reigns (14, 17) over those who are only children of Adam. Why are all guilty (12)?

The second Adam   5 : 12–21

Write down a point-by-point contrast between Adam and Jesus. How are they alike (compare Luke 3:38)? What are the entrance requirements of the new humanity as contrasted with the old? What replaces death? Meditate on verse 17 and try to think about what it means to 'reign in life through the one man Jesus Christ'.

Why not sin even more?   6 : 1–23 (1–14)

It's not a bad question if where sin abounds grace is that much more abundant. The crux of Paul's answer is that as death is the end of life, our union with Christ implies an end to the former way of life. What new alternative is now open to us? Notice carefully that verse 7 could not mean that we can expect sinlessness. Why (verses 12–15)? How do verses 1–11 help us to obey verses 12–14?

Who is your master?   6 : 1–23 (15–23)

These words contain the important truth that no-one is completely free. I am either a slave of sin or a slave of righteousness. What are the wages our former master pays? What gift can we expect from our new master? What is the responsibility of any slave (17)? Is there any sin which still seems to be your master? Let verse 16 convince you of your responsibility for yielding to it. What solution to the problem does verse 19 offer?

Death to the law   7 : 1–24 (1–6)

This passage provides a good opportunity to apply the 'analogy of Scripture', i.e. consulting other clear passages to understand the true meaning. This passage forces us to ask, What does it mean to be dead to the law? Try to discern the answer by studying the following passages:
  Matthew 5:17–18; Romans 10:3–4; Galatians 3:1–29; 5:13–26.

The law of sin still lives   7:1–24 (7–24)
Paul has just argued that the Christian is free from sin (as a master) and free from the law (as a way of justification). Does he mean to imply that the law is sin? Who is the real culprit that causes Paul such torment? Notice that Paul uses 'law' in three senses: the law of God (7, 9, 12, 14, 16), a generally observed fact (21), and an active principle within (23, 25). How does Paul use the word 'sin'? By 'flesh' he means here not the soft parts of the body, but the old nature, that which is opposed to the Spirit. Is Paul's frustration a Christian experience? Could a non-Christian write verse 22? Notice the shift in tenses between verses 13 and 14. Why is Paul wretched, even as a Christian? Is it not because of *himself* that he is unable to exercise the freedom which he has been granted?

The law of the Spirit   7:25—8:17 (7:25—8:8)
Trying to live the Christian life in one's own strength is a recipe for frustration. Human will, determination, effort, are, in themselves, no weapons against the 'law of sin'. What is the greater 'law' available to us (2)? What is the choice Paul sets before us? What are the consequences of the two paths? How do we 'walk according to the spirit' (4–8)?

The Spirit gives life   7:25—8:17 (8:9–17)
Who has the Spirit? What can we expect the Spirit to do? Compare verse 13 with Galatians 5:16–18. How do we co-operate with the Spirit to put to death the deeds of the body (compare Galatians 6:7–9)? What are the duties and privileges of being fellow heirs with Christ?

Three groaners   8:18–27
Creation groans, we groan, even the Spirit groans. Try to determine the reasons why. What are we waiting for? How does that certain hope affect life here and now? How does the Spirit help our prayers? Does this passage have anything to say about natural disasters?

What do we know for sure?   8:28–39 (28–30)
This paragraph describes God's activity as it relates to his purpose for us. What is God doing (28)? What things are as good as

done (30)? What is the purpose behind it all? What is our responsibility if we are to appropriate his promise (compare John 14:21)? Sonship is something we have (8:15–16) but also something we grow into (8:29).

Father, thank you for working to make us like Jesus. Teach us to grow in love for you.

What shall we say?   8:28–39 (31–39)
This is one of the most glorious passages in the whole New Testament. Instead of answering questions from this page, try to answer those Paul asks. What is his answer? Meditate again on verse 31. Could God withhold any good thing after giving what was dearest to him? Make some bold request of God in prayer.

Is God unjust?   9:1–29
Romans 9–11 needs to be studied as a unit. Try to take a whole morning, afternoon or evening to read and re-read these three chapters until you have the feel of Paul's argument.
    Take some time on this part of the section and answer the questions stated or implied by the text itself. Writing out your findings will probably help you get them more clearly in mind. Why did Paul need to assert that the word of God has not failed (6)? How does he support his claim? Is there injustice on God's part (14)? Why does God still find fault (19)?

How not to find righteousness   9:30–10:4
What two ways of justification does Paul discuss? Is zeal for God (2) enough? What else is needed? Why did Israel fail to find righteousness (3)? How did this wrong approach spoil their attitude toward Christ? Could you apply the principle to other religions? In what sense is Christ 'the end of the law' (remember 7:7–12)?

One way of salvation for everyone   10:5–13
Paul quotes Moses because Moses recognized that within the law was provision for obedience and forgiveness—that obedience is the way to life. The trouble seems to be that the Pharisees tried to use it as a human tool to establish their own

141

righteousness before God rather than as a guide for those who trusted God and wanted to follow him. Paul goes on to borrow some of Moses' words to describe saving faith. How would you describe it? What does this passage say about 'secret faith' or 'blind faith' (compare verse 3) or restricting faith to one race (12, 13)?

Faith's object   10 : 14–21
Trace the steps in bringing someone to salvation. Where do you think you fit in? What is implied about the object of faith? Verse 17 emphasizes that saving faith is faith in the risen Jesus. What light might this shed on the thorny problem of the salvation of the unevangelized? What do verses 18–21 imply about our responsibility as those who proclaim Christ?

That God may have mercy on all   11 : 1–36
This chapter faces squarely the embarrassing obser-vation—that God seems to have rejected his chosen people. Look at verses 29–32 as the key. God, who is absolutely free, could not put himself in a position where he owed salvation to anyone. Take some time and try to trace Paul's argument. It may help if you discover the purpose of God's hardening of Israel and his eventual plan for the nation (26).

Paul worships God (33–36) because he has seen a glimpse of how God can allow Israel freedom and still use them as a tool for the salvation of the whole world, how Israel can be elect and yet still be recipients of God's grace, and how Gentiles can be the first to receive the gospel and yet be in no position to boast.

Now what?   12 : 1–21 (1–13)
We have just explored some glorious truths about salvation. Its breadth and depth are beyond our minds' reach because God is its author. But we have not been called to sit amazed at its beauty but to reflect God's glory by living it out. It's a beautiful picture, but the question is, Where do I fit in? Look at these verses with one question in mind: What does it mean to think rightly about myself? Follow out as many implications as you can. Notice that we are to think of ourselves in terms of the gifts God has given us, so that the service we render him may be acceptable.

142

Doing good 12 : 1–21 (14–21)
Let no-one think for a moment that justification by faith allows us to minimize the place of good works. Verse 21 is the principle which applies not only in these cases but many others. Does verse 20 tell us to do something good to enemies in order that something bad might happen to them (compare Matthew 5:44)? What good thing could be implied by 'heaping burning coals upon his head'?

Relating to government 13 : 1–14 (1–7)
What are the duties of governing authorities? Where do they get their authority? What should we do as those under government? The next question is difficult but it must be faced. What happens when a government ceases to function as God's servant, and punishes good and rewards evil? Is there a clue in this passage? How do we answer such questions?

Love and the law 13 : 1–14 (8–14)
Those who believe in 'situation ethics' claim to follow the radical requirements of love even when it occasionally means doing what the Bible calls wrong. They would claim for instance that love may make adultery or murder 'right' in certain circumstances. How could you use this passage to help someone see the weakness of such a position? How does the passing of time act as a further stimulus to right living (compare 1 John 3:3)?

When it's a matter of opinion 14 : 1–23
This passage deals not with black and white moral issues but with those in the grey area. That is important to see. Otherwise words like those in verse 14 contradict practically the whole of the rest of Scripture. There are two types of people (2), and two temptations (3, 10, 13). You can be a 'weak brother' on some issues and not on others. What principles can you discover which help us not to judge or despise others?

A word of encouragement 15 : 1–33 (1–13)
If we seriously take Christ as our example, how will we deal with others (2, 7)? How does the encouragement of the Old

Testament produce hope in those who live in the days after the coming of Jesus (4–6, 13)?

A satisfied apostle   15 : 1–33 (14–29)
What seem to be the marks of the Roman Christians which led Paul to commend them so highly? Notice that, as spiritual as they were, they were not above further instruction, even in the very basics of the faith.

Why could Paul be proud of his work for the gospel? What legitimate generalizations could be made from Paul's comments about his own ministry?

An appeal and an expectation   15 : 1–33 (29–33)
You may have thought that the preceding passage sounded a bit presumptuous despite the disclaimers. These verses erase any such impression. Prayer is the real indicator of where our trust lies. Paul's assurance of usefulness to the saints was confidence in God, not in himself. How does verse 32 complete this picture?

Person to person   16 : 1–23 (1–16)
Resist the temptation to think that this letter ended with chapter 15! The presence of these greetings implies a great deal. For example, Paul knew many of his readers personally, and didn't miss the opportunity to spur them on to do good works and to encourage others by their example. What does Paul tend to commend? Do you think that in Romans Paul was proclaiming the gospel to his family (compare his references to his 'kinsmen' and 'mother')? What traditional barriers seem to have been broken down?

Be wise   16 : 1–23 (17–23)
How, according to Paul, should we relate to those who oppose apostolic doctrine? Why? Notice that Paul does not treat the Romans' well-known obedience as a permanent endowment which cannot be altered. What can we learn from that observation? How do we apply the promise of verse 20?

The obedience of faith   16 : 25–27
What was Paul's purpose in writing this letter, and what's the

point of our reading it? Paul agrees with himself (compare 1:5): it is to bring about the obedience of faith. We are to believe and obey what we have heard. God commands it; he enables us to do it; he is glorified by it.

Father, use this letter and what I have learned from it to make me more like Jesus and so more like you.

Forgive me for allowing myself to be conformed to this world and for accepting in myself that which is an unacceptable sacrifice to you.

Sanctify me by your Spirit, so that I may be able to put to death all those things in me that are part of the old life, and come alive even more fully with the new life you have given me in Jesus.

Continue always to thrill my mind with your gospel, and rejoice my heart with your mercy, so that I may always say of you with Paul:

'O the depth of the riches and wisdom and knowledge of God! How unsearchable are his judgments and how inscrutable his ways!

For from him and through him and to him are all things. To him be glory for ever. Amen.'

Deriving ethical principles from the Bible

No-one claims that the Bible is a list of do's and don'ts, but it does have much to say about behaviour. As God's Word, what it teaches must be taken as normative by those who want to follow God. Here are a few guidelines:

1 Try to come to Scripture empty-handed. Expect it to speak God's word and be willing to submit to it rather than using or even adjusting the Bible to justify yourself. Listen to this classic example of the latter, from an article by Richard Kirken: 'If the love of gay people for each other (including the much-desired pair binding) does not seem to fit into the scheme of past Judeo-Christian experience or insight, we must . . . adjust our outlook, framework and ethic so that they encourage total personal fulfilment within the gayness given to us by God.' That is the *wrong* approach!

2 Expect what the Bible teaches about morality and behaviour to mirror the character of God and to foster growth into the likeness of Jesus (Romans 8:29; Ephesians 4:13; 5:1; Colossians 3:1–17).

3 Recognize that love never dictates behaviour that is contrary to God's law, but always beyond it (Galatians 5:22, 23; 1 John 3:4–10, 23, 24; Romans 13:8–10).

4 Ask yourself what kind of behaviour is pleasing to the Lord (Ephesians 5:10, 11; Colossians 1:10).

5 Look for direct and specific statements about what is right and what is wrong (*e.g.* the Ten Commandments, the teaching of Jesus, the letters written to instruct the churches, *etc*). Biblical ethics claim to be eternal and therefore should not be lightly dismissed as simply cultural and therefore dispensable. On the other hand, an eternal principle (such as submission to authority) may have a cultural expression (such as wearing a head-covering). In that case, our duty is to obey the commandment in terms of our own culture.

6 Try to examine all the passages on a particular subject. Use a concordance or topical Bible or Bible dictionary.

2. Ethics: knowing and doing what is right

What is the Christian ethic? What does the Bible teach us to do? Jesus summarized the entire Old Testament ethic in two great commandments: love God with all your heart, soul and mind, and love your neighbour as yourself. Some people think we need say nothing more. But Jesus never intended these two great commandments to replace more specific ones. On the contrary, it is by keeping the commandments that we demonstrate our love for God and man (John 14:21; 1 John 4:20, 21). So specifics are important. The purpose of these studies is to help you think about specific moral issues and practices. It won't take you long to notice that some ethical questions have clear biblical answers, whereas others are never mentioned in Scripture. In these cases, the general teaching and outlook of the Bible must be applied to the specific situation. You will get the idea as we go along. Take these studies at your own speed and ask God to help you to obey his Word.

Speaking the truth
Look up these passages and read them in context: Exodus 20:16; Leviticus 19:11, 12 (what reason is given?); Ephesians 4:25; Colossians 3:9; 1 Timothy 1:10; John 14:6.

Commands to avoid lying and speak the truth are numerous, but speaking the truth has always been difficult. Even Abraham failed to tell the truth—on two separate occasions (Genesis 12:10–16; 20:1–18). Notice the excuses he offers and how his son Isaac learnt from his example (Genesis 26:6–11). What about the Israelite midwives who lied to Pharaoh in order to save the baby Jewish boys (see Exodus 1:15–22)? It seems to be a case of civil disobedience, choosing to obey God rather than man. God commends the midwives not for lying but for fearing God. Lying, even if it is the lesser of two evils, is still evil.

Poverty

Surely the way in which we Christians respond to the glaring fact of poverty should be different from the way the rest of the world responds to it. God, who is Spirit, is nevertheless intensely concerned about material things. Study these passages with an open mind, asking God to help you obey him.

Causes of poverty: Proverbs 6:10, 11; 13:18, 14:23; 19:15; 21:5; 21:17; 24:30–34; 28:19; but also Proverbs 13:23; 22:16; 30:13, 14; 2 Corinthians 8:2.

God's attitude towards poverty: Job 34:19; Psalm 9:18; Psalm 140:12; Proverbs 16:8; 19:22; 22:2; 28:6.

Our response to poverty and God's punishment or reward: Proverbs 11:25; 14:21; 14:31; 17:5; 19:17; 21:13; 21:26; 22:16; 22:22, 23; 28:8; 28:27; 29:7.

A wise man's prayer: Proverbs 30:8, 9.

Our Lord's example: 2 Corinthians 8:9.

The sanctity of life

War, starvation, abortion, euthanasia, 'the ethics of the lifeboat'—these subjects are constantly being discussed. One often feels that the primary considerations which lead people to adopt certain positions are survival, convenience and practicality. Some speak in terms of human worth, but define this worth solely in terms of productivity. Others—without any conspicuous logic—affirm with one breath that man has infinite value, and with the next describe him as the product of time and chance. If Christians are to contribute anything to the debate about these topics, we must think more clearly and have a much firmer foundation for our conclusions.

Why do we believe that life is valuable? Study the following passages in context (they do not exhaust the biblical teaching on these vexed ethical issues; they just begin to fill in the background so that we can begin to think about them in a Christian way):

1 God is the source of life. Man is created in his image: Genesis 1:26, 27; 2:7; Psalm 100:3; Isaiah 64:8; 42:5; Acts 17:25; Job 33:4.

2 God sustains life and takes it away according to his own sovereignty: Acts 17:28; Job 12:10; 27:3; 34:14, 15; Psalm 104:27–30; Matthew 6:26; Genesis 6:17; Deuteronomy 32:39; Judges 13:3.

3 Murder is prohibited. (The fact that death is penalty for murder and for other sins reflects not the cheapness of life, but God's hatred of sin and man's responsibility.) Exodus 20:13; 21:14, 29; Genesis 4:8–24, 9:5, 6; Leviticus 24:21; Deuteronomy 19:11–13; Matthew 5:21, 22; Romans 13:9, 10; 1 Timothy 1:9.

4 Jesus died so that people might experience life in all its fullness: John 10:10; 3:16. He died for sinners (Romans 5:8) to show how highly God values people even before they become his children.

5 Death is an enemy which takes away the possibility of repentance: Luke 16:19–31; 1 Corinthians 15:26; 2 Peter 3:9.

Violence

Are force and anarchy the way to accomplish peace and justice? Some people think so—apparently even some Christians. What is God's attitude? Look up 'violence' in a large concordance and study all the passages cited. Draw your own conclusions and think about what God requires of us today. Before you have finished your study, you should be formulating answers to some of these questions: What is violence? When is it legitimate? Does Jesus allow violence? What results can we expect from violence? What forms may non-violence take? If you are still unclear in your thinking, you might be helped by reading *A different dream: non-violence as practical politics* by Christopher Sugden (Grove Booklets, 1976).

Other ethical issues

Sometimes we may be called upon to give a Christian viewpoint on some particular practice, or, hearing what purports to be a Christian approach or practice, we may feel compelled to reply. If we are to do so faithfully, what we shall need is not a few texts at our fingertips — no doubt our opponents will cite a *few* — but a familiarity with the whole tone of Scripture in relation to the specific ethical problem. We too must cite biblical texts and take care not to disregard any part of biblical teaching. But we must learn to go back further to underlying principles. These we shall discover only by reading the Bible repeatedly with an eye open for statements which bear upon crucial issues, even if they do not mention them by name.

Useful background books

In our day it is inadmissable to complain at not receiving help in making the Bible come alive. There is a wealth of books written with great liveliness and a high standard of scholarship; they are usually easily available, but if any are out of print by the time you read this, you may be able to borrow them from a friend or library.

1 General

The Lion handbook to the Bible, ed. David and Pat Alexander (Lion, 1973)

Atlas of the Bible, L. H. Grollenberg (Nelson, 1956)

Understanding the Bible, John Stott (SU, 1972)

The new Bible dictionary, ed. J. D. Douglas *etc.* (IVP, 1972)

I believe in revelation, Leon Morris (Hodder and Stoughton, 1975)

In understanding be men, T. C. Hammond (IVP, 1968)

The Bible and archaeology, J. A. Thompson (Paternoster, 1973)

2 Old Testament

Let's read the Old Testament, Raymond Brown (Victory Press, 1971)

The message of the Old Testament, H. L. Ellison (Paternoster, 1969)

Israel and the nations, F. F. Bruce (Paternoster, 1973)

Men spake from God, H. L. Ellison (Paternoster, 1966)

The goodness of God, J. W. Wenham (IVP, 1974)

3 New Testament

The man they crucified, R. T. France (IVP, 1975)

The birth of the New Testament, C. F. D. Moule (A. and C. Black, 1966)

The New Testament: its background, growth and content, Bruce M. Metzger (Lutterworth, 1970)

New Testament history, F. F. Bruce (Oliphants, 1971)

The life and times of Jesus the Messiah, Alfred Edersheim (Pickering and Inglis, 1959)

3. True and false: the message of Jeremiah

The context 2 Kings 22—25 ;
2 Chronicles 34 : 1—36 : 21

Jeremiah is a magnificent book. Besides recounting the life and times of a highly courageous man of God, it shows us inside the spiritual life of this man and his relationship with God. It also handles, in the living crises of real history, many of the great issues with which God is concerned: the roots of social evil, the nature of true faith, the perversion of religion, the responsibilities of nations and rulers. This study divides the book into large sections, on each of which you can spend as many sessions as you need to explore the main themes to your own satisfaction, and without rushing.

Jeremiah's time was a day of decline (see History, p. 160) in which his spokesmanship for God was a lonely and costly business. Internally, the godless and immoral reign of Manasseh had been followed by the nondescript reign of Amon; the southern kingdom of Judah lay spiritually aimless, morally lax, and politically adrift. Externally, the old nutcracker situation between Egypt to the south-west and Assyria to the north-east was complicated by roving hordes to the north and Babylon's rising threat in the east.

Jeremiah's work fell mainly in the reigns of Josiah, Jehoiakim and Zedekiah, and so coincided with three differing phases in the decline of Jerusalem. Josiah's reign (from 639 BC) was one of largely unavailing reform, which Jeremiah supported while criticizing its superficiality. Jehoiakim's was a story of political deviousness and religious complacency, cut short by the Babylonian siege in which Ezekiel and others were deported. Zedekiah's was the last headlong rush into disaster. Jeremiah, whose condemnation of Jehoiakim's Judah was unrelieved, nevertheless began to mingle words of hope from God with his unyielding despair for the regime as it stood.

It will pay you to build your own timetable, from 2 Kings, 2 Chronicles and background books, into which to fit Jeremiah. What were the main features of Josiah's reform? Who felt its pressure? Do Kings and Chronicles take different viewpoints?

The call

The book of Jeremiah contains three main strands: accounts of Jeremiah's life and work by his assistant Baruch, records of the prophet's own words, and insights into his deep relationship with God. It is this last strand which gives the book its intensely personal nature. Jeremiah's calling was momentous and became the cornerstone of his certainty that God was with him as his lonely, unpopular ministry developed.

Jeremiah's call from God came in the reign of King Josiah in 626 BC. Josiah, a man of about Jeremiah's age, had become king at the age of eight in 639. Around the time of Jeremiah's call he was initiating a programme of reform against the kingdom's idolatry and consequent immorality. This was to be greatly sharpened in focus by the rediscovery of the book of the law (something like our Deuteronomy) in the temple in 621. No doubt Jeremiah's apprehension at the call grew largely from knowing what kind of time God's prophet would have in such circumstances.

Notice the role of *the word of God* in its several occurrences in this chapter; compare verses 1–3 with Luke 3: 1–3, and note which name matters in each case! How much of this chapter is purely personal to Jeremiah's biography, and how far does it teach general truth about God's foreknowledge and providence, and his dealings with his spokesman? Verse 10 is virtually a technical description of clearing an overgrown bombsite for building; how far is today's preacher or teacher under the same commission?

One feature of Jeremiah is the use of plays upon words, the first being in verses 11 and 12. Because the almond blossomed early, its Hebrew name meant the watch-tree, or waker-tree. Can we apply to today's situation the belief that God uses pagan nations to discipline his own people? Isn't such a line open to political abuse?

For Jeremiah, this was only the first in a series of interchanges with God which grew more poignant as his painful ministry developed. These are collected on page 157, and it may be worth reading that now to see more of his inner spiritual life before looking further at his work.

The opening message

These chapters come from the reign of Josiah, probably before Jeremiah was a very prominent figure, and they deal with the same issues as Josiah was seeking to tackle in his reforms. Jeremiah seems to have encouraged the reforms while criticizing the people for keeping them so superficial. Take a little time to analyse the whole section for yourself, absorbing its message and breaking it down into sections according to content.

Jeremiah seems to have agreed with Josiah that morality was not the root of the problem: religion was. Infidelity to God led on to ugly fruits of personal and social wrongdoing. Can you follow the metaphor of infidelity and its implications through this section? What kind of relationship does a charge of infidelity imply? What specific moral symptoms are mentioned as resulting from this religious disease? What, in practice, did Jeremiah want to see instead of the current situation?

Most of chapter 3 is given to showing how the northern kingdom of Israel should have been an example and a warning to southern Judah. How was this? In what way was she *less* blameworthy than the south? Loving promises for Israel now appear—implying what?

It is probably true that chapters 5 and 6 fall after the main thrust of Josiah's reforms, and are concerned to stress their lack of impact. This helps to explain the heightened tone of indignation. How does this compare with the impression given in 2 Kings and 2 Chronicles?

Three further themes are worth exploring. (i) As foreseen in chapter 1, God was planning to send 'evil from the north' to judge his people. At this stage these northerners are still a vague, though fearsome, threat; what will characterize their judging work, and how can God make them his agents? (ii) The responsibility of the leaders of the nations is a persistent theme throughout the book, with both political and religious leadership in mind. What is said about their behaviour, standards and role? How do they come to be associated with the falsity in religion which Jeremiah condemns? (iii) Where are the growing-points in Jeremiah's own relationship with God?

False religion
7–10, 23, 26

From this point on the exact chronological order of the book is not entirely clear. Probably most of chapters 7–20 belong to Jehoiakim's reign, and this makes up the main collection of Jeremiah's own sayings (chapters 1–20) which may well correspond to the roll dictated to Baruch (see chapter 36). Chapter 26 gives the historical context: it is the beginning of Jehoiakim's reign, and Jeremiah now becomes a major and troublesome public figure as he steps out in the temple of Jerusalem, the very heart of the nation, to warn against the people's glib self-confidence. Whatever had provoked Josiah's foolish attempt to stand in the way of Pharaoh Neco at Megiddo, there was every reason to expect fierce reprisals. When the Pharaoh was content with removing the new king Jehoahaz after three months and putting in the puppet Eliakim (renamed Jehoiakim) it must have seemed that Judah's God was smiling sweetly (see 2 Kings 23:28–37).

Jeremiah was sent to assail any such comfortable notion. God was not to be domesticated by any automatic and outward formal means while his law and will were disregarded. None of God's gifts to the people was a guarantee of safety by itself, when treated as a good luck charm or separated from obedience. Five separate examples are given in these chapters—the temple, the city of Jerusalem, the sacrifices, the law itself and the prophets; gather the references to each. What was the point of referring to Shiloh?

Draw out in detail the contrast between idols and the true God in chapter 10. What else does Scripture say about idolatry? 'Shepherds' in 10:21 is a common biblical term for leaders, used much in this book as well as in the history books, psalms and other prophets. What light does this shed on the New Testament's usage?

Among the shepherds were the official prophets, whom Jeremiah lambasts in chapter 23. How could they have slid into this position of untruth? What were the pressures on them? How should they have known the real 'burden of the Lord'? How could a similar phenomenon show up today?

Opposition

It was hardly to be expected that Jeremiah's efforts would escape a hostile reaction, but the bitterest blow came from the hostility of his own family (see chapter 1:1 and chapter 11:18—12:6). Anathoth, Jeremiah's home, lies a few miles north of Jerusalem and reappears in the story in chapter 32. There is no particular evidence that Jeremiah was himself a priest, though he may have been destined for that until God intervened; either way his aristocratic priestly family was acutely embarrassed by his prophetic message. This was sharpened by the unheard-of decision not to marry (chapter 16). Reflect on the many biblical parallels and the ways in which they do and do not apply to today's Christian.

What effect do you think his priestly background had upon Jeremiah's own outlook and thinking? (You may need to do some homework on the Jewish priesthood from the background books.) A useful comparison is Jeremiah's contemporary, the prophet Ezekiel, who was also of a priestly line and seems to have longed for the priest's work which he was denied by the exile in Babylon: God made it up to him by calling him as a prophet in the precise year when he would have qualified for the priesthood.

One well-known feature of Ezekiel's work was his prophecies acted out in dramatic form, and there are also several of these in Jeremiah. The story of the loincloth (chapter 13) may be the first of these, though the distances involved (two round trips of 800 miles) suggest that this was a visionary journey akin to Ezekiel chapter 8.

A great deal emerges from the very intimate exchanges between Jeremiah and the Lord, sometimes called his 'complaints' (see the next section). There are several in this section; what do they tell us about Jeremiah himself, his experience, his work, and the way God supported him? What light do they shed on the nation's revolt as a whole (chapter 13), the Anathoth plot (chapters 11 and 12), the conflict with the priests and prophets (chapter 14), the cost of faithful service (chapter 15)?

Support

In the context of his society, what was the point of God's command to Jeremiah not to marry? What were the consequences for him?

The establishment's opposition to Jeremiah comes to a head with the story of Pashur. Who were the wise who lined up with prophets and priests in 18:18? What, if any, are today's equivalents of these three? How had their attitudes become perversions of God's purpose?

Like the watch-tree and the rotten loin-cloth, the picture of God the potter reasserts God's control despite any opposition. But how can the pot of the nation be smashed in judgment (chapter 21) if God is responsible for its being the way it is? The potter's control is not confined to one nation; he has a broader purpose for the world (end of chapter 16). Is this wider vision characteristic of Jeremiah so far and of the Old Testament in general? Watch for it in the rest of the book.

One helpful way of studying Scripture is to think how you would explain it to others, *e.g.* in a sermon or young people's talk. You may like to try this with chapter 17:5–8.

As this is probably the last section of Jeremiah's own scroll (see chapter 36), this is the moment to review his own relationship with God as expressed here. In a way everything sheds light on this, but these passages highlight it:

1:1–19; 4:13–18; 7:16–20; 27–34; 8:18—9:3; 10:23–25; 11:14—12:6; 13:1–17; 14:13–18; 15:10–21; 16:1–4; 17:14–18; 18:18–23; 2-:7–18.

How do these passages in this section (chapters 16–20) add to the previous picture? How does God reassure and strengthen his servant in the face of hostility? How does he deal with Jeremiah's self-pity? Does it matter that the story ends on a cry of pain, not of praise and victory? Is it correct or helpful to see Jesus prefigured in Jeremiah's experience—and if so, how?

True leadership

Two problems arise here. The first is that after chapter 20, Jeremiah's book is a compilation in which not even the narrative parts are in order; secondly we are plunged further into the bewildering history of the period. We try to meet both problems in the 'History' section (p. 160).

For the moment we are concerned with the fourfold cluster of thoughts about leadership in these eight chapters. First, God addresses the kings through Jeremiah in chapters 21, 22, 26, and 27; that includes Jehoiakim and Zedekiah, with some reference to Jehoahaz (Shallum) and Jehoiachim (Coniah). What is the essence of God's message to them? What are the basic elements of their failures? How far were they right in accusing Jeremiah of sedition?

We have already touched on the leadership given by the prophets; here the debate comes into the open in chapters 23, 27, 28 and 29. Of course it was always difficult for the ordinary person to judge who really was God's spokesman and who was not; what criteria might he use? What were the problems of being an 'official' prophet on the establishment payroll, as many were? We tend to think that Christians should conduct debates with tact and courtesy, but Jeremiah and Hananiah collided very bluntly. What is the place of confrontation and controversy among God's people? How much is it a matter of personality?

A third area of leadership concerned the exile in Bablyon, and this debate arose from the previous one. If Jeremiah was right, then leaders in exile should set the example of settling down and keeping life going there; if he was wrong, they should keep the people's bags packed for return. This is a question of how to assess God's hand in history and how best to act in accordance with it. How do similar conflicts arise in our own day? In this case God spoke vividly (chapter 24) but still left Jeremiah to battle out the issues (chapter 29). This is where Ezekiel's message is relevant from the other end.

The fourth area concerns wider issues than Judah, as God speaks to the nations in general (chapter 25). Their leaders, too, are responsible to him. Jeremiah returns to this theme below (see the section on 'The nations', p. 161).

Promise

Some people still think of Jeremiah as a pessimist, but these chapters are no 'jeremiad'! The situation rightly called God's condemnation from his prophet's lips—but here, as so often, God lifts the curtain on a hopeful future even before the heaviest blow of judgment has fallen. Some of this clearly comes during imprisonment in Zedekiah's reign, and most of it probably belongs to this time.

What are the roles in which God describes his own action? What relationships with the people do they imply, and how do these relate to the earlier messages of challenge and judgment? Collect the passages which make promises specifically about the city, the covenant, and the kingship.

What are the covenants in the Bible? What was their history before Jeremiah? What is novel about the promised *new* covenant?

The words about promised kings fit into a wider Old Testament hope for a leader who would fulfil the ideal from which all the kings of history had fallen short. Where are the other main texts about this? How far are these words of Jeremiah messianic predictions?

The specific theme of rebuilding appears in chapter 31; what is this fulfilling?

The incident of the land at Anathoth is another living parable. Such family inheritances never went on to the open market, but members of the family had rights of purchase in a certain order. Jeremiah's purchase, in the blackest days for Jerusalem, was a sign: although these were classic days for pessimism in the property market, the prophet was declaring his confidence in a rich future for the land because God was protecting it and had spoken of his plans to restore it. Why is Jeremiah's cry of praise significant? What does it add to our knowledge of his relationship with God?

Much of this took place in prison. Which of God's other servants have found themselves in this position and how did it affect them, their message, and God's work?

The later part of Jeremiah is difficult to follow because of the complex history it recounts and the unhistorical order in which the writing was compiled. To sort out the account itself, the narrative passages should probably be taken in roughly this order: 26; 35; 36; 24; 29; 27; 28; 21; 34:1–7; 37:1–10; 34:8–22; 37:11–21; 32; 33; 38:1–28a; 39:15–18; 38:28b—39:14; 40–44. The messages of chapters 22 and 23 fit into the early part (up to Jehoiachin); those of 30 and 31 probably fit into Zedekiah's reign.

The outline story is this. When Josiah was killed at Megiddo in 609 BC he was briefly succeeded by Jehoahaz (that is, Shallum; 22:10–12). The Egyptians then imposed a puppet king, Eliakim, renamed Jehoiakim, who became the second main figure with whom Jeremiah had to deal. Most of chapters 7–20 have referred to his reign, as do chapters 22, 23, 26, 35 and 36. On the broader scene the Babylonians had finally taken the capital of Assyria, Nineveh, in 612, and defeated the Egyptians at Carchemish in 605. This meant that Jehoiakim had to transfer his allegiance to Babylon, and in fact it was his reversal to Egypt's fold in 598 which brought the wrath of Babylon on his head in the siege of Jerusalem. The next year Jehoiakim died during the siege, and his son Jehoiachin succeeded, only to be taken into exile with Ezekiel and other leading figures when the city fell (he is the Coniah of 22:24–30). Zedekiah, who succeeded as Babylon's vassal king, was much in the mould of his predecessors and hardly drew Jeremiah's favour. His attempt at an Egyptian alliance led to the sack of Jerusalem and a mass exile which left a largely deserted Jerusalem under the governership of Gedaliah; the story from here on is told fairly clearly in later chapters.

We owe much to Baruch; what kind of portrait emerges from chapters 36 and 45? What do we learn from the Rechabites? How far does spiritual influence inevitably involve God's spokesmen with secular leaders, and how might Jeremiah's dealings with Zedekiah inform our praying for today's church leaders? What does the incident in chapter 43 teach about God's guidance?

The nations
These last chapters (with the exception of chapter 52, which is a historical summary drawn from 2 Kings) contain a series of messages from God for the surrounding nations. How far is his judgment of them due to their attacks on Israel or Judah, and how far is it just because they have done wrong? In other words, are they condemned for opposing God's specific plan of salvation via the promised land, or for failing in their human responsibilities to him as God? What would be the implications of the two lines of thought?

What in particular are the things in which they have mistakenly put their trust? What are the modern equivalents? What responsibilities of national leaders emerge?

Babylon especially is taken to task, but is this fair? How can God judge Babylon when he said himself that Babylon was raised up as his weapon to judge Jerusalem? Jeremiah seems to hold both Babylon and the Jews responsible for the ruin of Jerusalem. Does that make sense?

Much of this section is bloodthirsty. How can this be the voice of God?

If you were in a position of national leadership today, what message from God might you be seeking to convey? How could you do it with urgency, credibility and compassion?

In conclusion, try to summarize the main truths and emphases you have learnt from Jeremiah. Go back over specific details or individual texts which have struck you personally. How will the study affect your behaviour and attitudes, and the plans and ambitions of your future?

A word about Lamentations
Despite some traditions, these polished poetic dirges over the fall of Jerusalem are almost certainly unconnected with Jeremiah. They still offer a deep expression of grief, especially the grief of God's people over the ruin of his work; as such they can rightly give us insight into the grief of Christ.

Group Bible study

Alongside systematic personal study, there is a particular value in studying the Bible in a group. For this reason many churches and Christian Unions give such groups high priority in their programmes. A group of people can see round a subject or a problem in a way that no individual can; so the individual can gain from the insights of others in a group and from their help with difficult passages. It also helps for a group which is working together in worship, service or evangelism to study together and bring the Bible's view to bear on their joint activities. Such a group can be a microcosm of the local church, giving an opportunity for worship, prayer, friendship and support, as well as for Bible study itself.

It can be helpful to link your personal study to that of the group, to give greater depth and background to the group study. Often, however, it is sufficient to give one day a week to this (say the day when the group is to meet) and reserve most of one's time for different study to keep the group's in perspective.

Leading a group study is a privilege and worth doing well. Try to go on a short course on how to do it; if there isn't one, get your church or CU to run one. The essentials are:

1 to prepare well, both getting to grips with the passage and preparing questions which will help the group to do so

2 to give everyone a chance to contribute, drawing out the quiet ones and sitting on the garrulous, and not delivering sermons oneself

3 to stick to the passage and not be diverted by chit-chat, red herrings, hobby-horses, or too many cross-references

4 to establish what the passage says, what it means, and how it applies in practice

5 to care for the group as a whole, praying for them and taking an interest in their lives and problems.

4. 2 Timothy, a pastor's letter: for group study

If learning from the Bible is a joy, helping others to learn from it is a greater one. Don't assume that teaching is limited to a few with special training. The writer to the Hebrews implies that becoming a teacher is the expected thing rather than the exception (Hebrews 5: 12).

In the next few studies, try to learn for yourself, but at the same time, think how you might help others learn some new truths too. Think of yourself not as a lecturer but a guide who always points people back to the text. One important step in becoming an effective leader is to learn to ask the right questions. They should be neither too easy, nor too hard, but should turn the other person back to the passage.

The gospel   chapter 1
Paul really wanted the best for Timothy and for the church. Notice that his comments begin with positive statements, are accompanied by prayer, and encourage Timothy to build on the gifts God has given him. These ingredients make the exhortation acceptable and effective.

Go through the passage with a fine-toothed comb and notice what God has given us in the gospel. What is the primary gift? How do we qualify to receive the good things God has for us? What other gifts are mentioned or implied? What responsibilities?

Could you summarize the gospel from this passage? How do we guard the gospel?

What is the alternative to faithfully taking one's share of suffering for the gospel?

For group study, decide what stands out in the passage. Does the personal pronoun 'I' give you any clues about where to start?

Suffering for the gospel   2: 1–19
Suffering for the gospel is more than idly taking your share of the bruises. It is purposeful, selfless living, which by its very

163

nature demands strength and discipline and entails suffering. What is the basic task to which we who have been given the gospel are called (2)? Look at each of the images (3–6). Obey verse 7 for a few minutes and write down your findings.

What is it that makes suffering worth while? What promises are there to claim in verses 11–13? What conditions must be met?

Why is our handling of the Bible so important? What are some of the pitfalls for teachers?

On what do we stand in the final analysis?

Go back over the passage and think what questions group members might ask. Instead of thinking up answers, discover ways of pointing them back to this passage and others.

Useful to the Master   2 : 20–26

Throughout this letter, Paul is drawing contrasts between the righteous and unrighteous, the faithful and the unfaithful. For the most part, he catalogues the results, but in this passage he sets before us a moral fork in the road, or, if you like, a watershed. One road leads to uselessness, the other to readiness for any good work for the Master. One drop of water flows into the reservoir of doing the devil's will; the other into that of purity and obedience.

Make a list of those things which we must studiously avoid. What, by contrast, are our goals?

Meditate on the metaphor of the vessels. You might ask your group, 'Why do you suppose Paul chose this particular metaphor?' What would summarize the most important quality and how do we attain it? Get group members to take specific action to obey the commandment here.

The folly of evil men   3 : 1–9, 13

Paul gives us a character sketch of evil men. He speaks of underlying motives, evident qualities, and actions. Then he mentions behaviour that is typical of such people. From the context, try to determine where they went wrong. What was their downfall? What can we learn about the nature of truth? What is to be our attitude toward such people? How can that be reconciled with the teaching of 2:24?

Write out a list of usable questions. Some should simply draw attention to facts, others should focus on explaining and relating the statements. Work back over your list to see that there is a balance of 'Who?', 'What?', 'Why?', and 'How?' questions.

To live a godly life   3 : 10–17

This passage seems to imply two means of learning for the Christian. How do they relate to each other and what do they imply for us as Christian leaders?

What does the fact that God 'breathed' Scripture tell us about the Bible? What is the purpose of Bible study? Does verse 16 give you any clues as to *how* to study the Bible? Write down any that come to mind.

Think about how Scripture equips us for *every* good work. This time, start from experience. Get your group members to share common objections to belief in the Bible. Then help them see why Paul trusted the Bible completely (compare Acts 24 : 14) and why we should.

As for you . . .   4 : 1–5

Yes, you say, but let's be practical! What am I actually supposed to do? Paul gives Timothy a very strong charge or commandment. Its basis is the nature of God and Christ and of the written Word. Its means of application is personal (2) and its fulfilling is sorely needed.

Notice who must share responsibility for sub-standard teaching and preaching.

Look at verse 2 to see what is required of us. Use a concordance or Bible dictionary to clarify the meaning of 'convince, rebuke, and exhort'. Encourage your Bible study group to think of some example of 'myths' into which some people have wandered (compare 2 : 18).

For example   4 : 6–22

As if Paul hadn't given enough personal examples to make this point, he speaks again of himself and then almost incidentally of others whose lives bear out all he has been saying—whether as positive examples or negative. What can those who imitate

165

Paul expect? What went wrong in the cases of those who deserted Paul?

How could you use this passage to get people to think seriously about heaven? What is a natural application of the truth exemplified by Paul's life?

5. Matthew and the kingdom: a Gospel and its emphases

It is extraordinary how unfamiliar one can be with the Gospels, and how vague our knowledge of these key writings often is.

The next series of studies is a detailed look at Matthew's Gospel. But though it covers the whole book, it is far from comprehensive. It majors on just one theme—the kingdom of God—as an illustration of how a Gospel can be approached. Some may feel that, in such an approach, the point has been laboured too much. We live in age of superficiality, however, where the depths often remain unexplored. This theme is just one of Matthew's particular interests. On a subsequent occasion it would be worth going through the whole Gospel with a different theme in mind (*e.g.* Old Testament allusions, the law, the disciples' faith, teaching for the church, *etc.*).

Some suggestions

1 Before doing the detail, read through the whole gospel at one sitting.
2 Buy or borrow from a library a commentary, such as:
   R. V. G. Tasker, *Matthew* (Tyndale New Testament Commentaries, IVP, 1971)
   David Hill, *The Gospel of Matthew* (New Century Bible, Oliphants, 1972)
3 Find out the background to the Gospel—its authorship, date, purpose and the geography of the events described.
4 Work hard at the questions asked in the following notes.
5 Do a careful study of:
   G. E. Ladd, *The Gospel of the kingdom* (Eerdmans, 1959)
   Jesus and the kingdom (SPCK, 1966).

The man born to be King

The genealogy and birth of the King   1:1–25

Right at the beginning Matthew presents this child as of kingly origin (from David) and as the Jewish Messiah (from Abraham). Compare this with Luke's presentation of Jesus as the representative man (from Adam). The presence of the genealogy warns us that we will not understand what follows except in the light of Old Testament history. The birth narrative is striking for its brevity, emphasizing (i) the Spirit's intervention (he began the world (Genesis 1:2), and is now forming the child to renew the world): (ii) Joseph as the righteous Jew (who knew enough biology to be embarrassed), and (iii) the significance of the name of Jesus.

The visit of the wise men   2:1–12

Though Matthew is writing the Jewish Gospel about their King (2), the new King has Gentile worshippers; and though the chief priests and scribes know where to find him they do not bother to go (? like modern leaders). Herod is motivated to go but gets others to do his work (compare the child King). The wise men's joy and worship are genuine and their gifts are not only significant—gold for royalty, incense for divinity, and myrrh for his bitter death—but also valuable for the long journey ahead for this particular family. Look up the references for verse 6—Micah 5:2 and 2 Samuel 5:2.

The escape to Egypt and return to Nazareth
2:13–23

The central theme of these verses is God's providential care of this child in fulfilment of the prophecies, for in spite of the terrible slaughter he is at work. What do you know about the different Herods in the biblical story? Do you know where and when they reigned? What do you make of the prophecy in verse 18? The original context of this quotation from Jeremiah 31 is one of hope. As Hill comments, 'The sorrow of the bereaved mothers (like the sorrow of Rachel for the Babylonian exile) was destined in the divine providence to result in great reward, the preservation of Jesus for his saving ministry.'

168

Foundations of the kingdom

The King is announced 3 : 1–12

The kingdom of God concerns his authority and power. Its imminence demands just one response—repentance. John's preaching caused a sensation, for there had been no prophet for 400 years. His role was preparatory; his task was to introduce the Messiah and to explode popular myths about him (*e.g.* that he was a national-social liberator). He focused on the individual, denounced hypocrisy (7, 8), and warned of false hopes (9, 10). His baptism was astonishingly new—once and for all, with a decisive turning to God (compare contemporary ritual baptisms, which were repetitive). His whole testimony is to Christ—what features of him does he highlight (11, 12)?

The King is humbled 3 : 13–17

In the light of John's teaching, the baptism of Jesus is the point of identification between the two ministries. John continues to point to Jesus; Jesus authenticates John's message. Entry into the kingdom is by baptism, and the beginning of the proclamation of the kingdom by Jesus is at his baptism. Though he needed no repentance, he took the sinner's place in this symbolic act which is an illustration of the greater baptism at Calvary (Mark 10:38, 39). If for us baptism is an outward and visible sign of an inward and spiritual reality, what was baptism for Jesus?

The King is tempted 4 : 1–11

The context is important; just after his ministry has had heavenly confirmation, easier ways than the cross (of which his baptism speaks) are suggested. What features of the devil's tactics can you identify as those which he uses today? Jesus faced three tests: (i) obedience (3, 4), where he was tempted to meet legitimate needs by illegitimate means; (ii) trust (5–7), where he could have demonstrated his kingship by a spectacular manifestation; (iii) loyalty (8–10), where the devil offered him compromise and co-operation. It is amazing to think of him—the Kings of kings—hungry, unnoticed and apparently powerless, but content to be so because he knew the Scriptures.

The beginning of the Galilean ministry   4:12–25

In fulfilment of the prophecy, the coming of the kingdom is for those in need (and those who know it). For them Christ brings 'life and immortality to light' (16). Note that his preaching (17) is not 'Repent, for the end is nigh'. Such a message would quickly be discredited; his actual message, though unrecognized by many, has the unassailable feature of being true! The kingdom is near. It is therefore a time of opportunity, a time of judgment, a time of decision. The King's authority commands obedience (20, 22), and his power is demonstrated (23, 24).

The teaching of the King

The King's people are happy   5:1–12

The happy people are Christian people, subjects of the kingdom, the ones who know their spiritual poverty (3) and are sensitive to their sin (4). They are unselfish (5), they mean business (6), and they know about mercy (7), purity (8) and peace (9). Such people invite antagonism (10–12), but such a reaction against them is a test of their reality. The teaching of Jesus about happiness is breath-taking in its originality—look up the other references, Matthew 11:6; 13:16; 24:46, and Luke 1:45; 11:27, 28; 14:14, 15. Two striking features are (i) their Christ-centredness, and (ii) their 'this-worldliness'. Can you find more?

The King's people are influential   5:13–16

People of the kingdom have a preserving power to them which makes them capable of stopping the rot in society. The preservation of society from destruction and degradation depends on the presence and potency of Christians (13). And just as the Christians have taken over from Judaism the role of 'savour' of the world, so they share in the mission of the Servant, to be 'a light to the nations' (Isaiah 42:6; 9:6). Look up Romans 2:19 and Philippians 2:15. Note that verse 16 is an exhortation, and that our light is a reflected glory. Is it true of your life today?

170

The King's people are righteous   5 : 17–26
The rules of the new kingdom which Jesus inaugurates are more, not less, exacting than the old ones. They are a fulfilment, not an abolition; a development, not a destruction (17–20). This means that we must know and obey the commands of the law and the injunctions of the prophets (even the least of them: 19)). Have you got to grips with the Old Testament yet? The antithesis introduced by 'You have heard that it was said. . .' is not between Jesus' teaching and Old Testament law. What is he objecting to (22)? What's the point of mentioning the two situations in verses 23–26?

The King's people are straightforward   5 : 27–37
It is easy to focus one's attention on the difficult problem of divorce (31, 32) but this demands a study of other passages and probably also help with exegesis,* so study it another time. The matters of sight (27–29) and speech (33–37) are nearer to home and daily living and are, in that sense, more important. The teaching is dramatic in verses 29 and 30, with a decisiveness that speaks volumes to our age of compromise. How are you going to apply it to your own life? Verse 34 does not refer to an oath in court (see 26:63, 64). Is your speech true?

The King's people are open-handed   5 : 38–48
The law of retaliation (38) was to curb revenge and to make restitution just. Subjects of the kingdom, though, must be ready to suffer loss; characteristically they are to be generous. Does verse 42 mean that all tramps and drop-outs should be given whatever they ask for? What other scriptures apply to that situation? 'Hate your enemy' is, of course, an unscriptural addition (43). What features of God's character are we to emulate (45)? What does verse 47 tell us about the sort of kingdom to which we belong? Confess your low standard and aim higher (48).

*e.g. D. Field, *Taking sides* (IVP, 1975); J. R. W. Stott, *Divorce* (Falcon, 1972).

Maintaining secrecy 6:1–6

Secrecy is a great Bible theme, and in an age when everything has to be open and exposed it's in great need of recovery. Piety is also a word that needs to be reclaimed. It has become a dirty word, but Jesus' objection is not to piety itself but to parading it publicly (1). Giving (2) and praying (5) are two good aspects of piety. The crucial question is not whether your private life bears public scrutiny, but does it bear God's scrutiny? Our public sham does not fool God, for he sees the secret things, so beware!

Maintaining simplicity 6:7–15

Long prayers may betray emptiness (7) though short ones may also betray the poverty of our relationship with God. Jesus' prayer is a model of content and brevity. It begins with God—his character and his concerns (9, 10), and it acknowledges our needs—food, forgiveness and protection (11–13)—and throughout it breathes a real conversation between a real Father and real children about the real world. Verses 14 and 15 continue with that uncomfortable note of reality. What is the pattern of your own praying? How does it need to be improved to approximate to this model?

Maintaining direction 6:16–24

Fasting, like giving and praying, is a Christian discipline and a matter between you and God (18). Spiritual capital really is of more value than earthly wealth; the latter is insecure but the former is beyond the ravages of moth, rust and thieves (19, 20). But the world still does not believe it! Why not (22, 23)? If a man's spiritual sense (his eye, 22) is healthy, his whole life will bear testimony to it; the reverse if it is diseased (23). Single-mindedness spells spiritual health; double-mindedness spells disaster (24). Some things are either/or, not both/and. Does your heart belong to the King (21)?

Maintaining composure 6 : 25–34

Bible 'therefores' are important; they are signals to make us read carefully in the light of the previous passage. What is the basis, then, from yesterday's reading, for leaving anxiety behind (25)? Which verse is today's passage confirms that theme? The answer to that question is the verse that emphasizes man's response. The passage as a whole, however, is a wonderful illustration of the balanced reasoning in the teaching of Jesus—the providential care of God should not lead to a *laissez-faire* attitude on our part, but to diligent action (33). Meditate on his works in creation and learn distinctive lessons (32).

Walking the King's way 7 : 1–12

Verse 1 is a warning against a censorious spirit, and not against a proper critical appraisal. The divine economy cannot be cheated, and justice will prevail (2). Hypocrisy will be seen for what it is—a selfishly motivated distortion of proportions (3–5). All this is to remind us that judgment, justice and a true sense of proportion belong to the King. But our King is generous (8) and wise (11) too! We are to walk in his ways with a discriminating mind (6, 9–11) and a generous heart (11). What do verses 7–11 teach us about prayer and God's nature?

Doing the King's will 7 : 13–29

Unpalatable teaching (13, 14)! Is there any way of making it more attractive? Many have tried and failed. The wide road is populated not only because the way is easy, but because there are many advocating it (15). Their identity, however, is not hidden from the observant (16–18). It is not lip-service which gains entrance (21), nor spectacular works (22), but moral obedience (21). It's amazing that this great section of Jesus' teaching ends with the illustration of a house crashing to the ground. Familiarity blinds us to the impact of this parable. Is your faith 'as safe as houses'? How do you know? Are you under the King's authority?

The announcement of the kingdom

The acts of the King 8 : 1–13

The authority of Jesus was not limited to teaching, but extended to healing. The dawn of the kingdom is heralded not only by authoritative words but also by authoritative deeds. Throughout the Bible, leprosy is used as a symbol of sin (compare Leviticus 13, 14). What features in this story (2–4) parallel the sinner's forgiveness? The second story speaks vividly of the victim's powerlessness (6), of the centurion's faith (8), and of Jesus' amazement (10). Verses 11 and 12 are very significant in the light of Matthew's interest in relating Jesus to the history of Israel, but it took time for the penny to drop.

The demands of the King 8 : 14–22

Note the absence of elaborate medical ritual (15, 16)—a touch and a word—and note the extent of his power. (16). Again Matthew knows that all this is *fulfilment* (17). Don't bypass the result of his work (15). Does service characterize your life today? The scribe is enthusiastic to follow Christ (19) but may not have understood the implications (20). The disciple wants to postpone commitment, not understanding the urgency of the situation (22). Are you naive in your enthusiasm, or are you blind to your obligation that the King's service comes first?

The power of the King 8 : 23–34

To the disciples' mind, they were at the mercy of the elements—there was no hope (25). And yet their question shows some faith (a 'little', 26) that his power may extend to the elements. It makes you think when his power so patently does extend that far (26, 27)!

Those who had caused terror for others (28) were now afraid themselves (29), for their defeat was imminent. The response of the city is tragic (34), more concerned with the loss of their property than with the wonderful news that mental derangement had been conquered. How does that apply today?

174

The dominion of the King   9 : 1–8

The human mind is contorted; the human heart is warped! Look at these scribes, who thought that Jesus' reign extended only to the physical and material world! Quack miracle workers have only quack remedies for sin. Jesus' authority is for real in both the physical and the spiritual realms (6); the two belong together. His extraordinary power demonstrated in ways that could be seen and verified physically give us confidence that he has power in the spiritual world too. He is Lord of both, and there is only one response to such wonderful news (8). Or do you remain in the camp of verse 4?

The company of the King   9 : 9–17

The simple description betrays a momentous decision (9). The tax collector was a despised quisling of the occupying Romans, but the news of the kingdom was for such as he (10). What do verses 12 and 13 tell us about entry into the kingdom? The Jews thought of the coming of the Messiah in terms of a marriage feast; mourning is not on at weddings! To what does verse 15b refer? The last two illustrations are remarkably apt when applied to the inauguration of the kingdom. Do you understand it? If not, wrestle with it first, then look up a commentary.

The response to the King   9 : 18–34

The King is the one who brings life from the dead (25), hope after years of suffering (20), sight to the blind (30) and words to the speechless (33). What good news! He is the great restorer, but although the power remains his and his alone, the work of restoration depends on our response of faith and trust (18, 21, 28, compare 24). All these stories illustrate spiritual truth; the earthly ministry of Jesus always illumines his heavenly one. Therefore what practical significance does verse 32 have for us today? What is Jesus' answer to verse 34?

The commission of the King 9:35—10:4

The ministry of Jesus was active and energetic (35) and his disciples were called to be dynamic too (1)! Supremely, he had an eye for the situation—the master observer (36). Both metaphors, one from the hillside and one from the field, were familiar to the disciples. But they probably hadn't seen the crowds in terms of harassment and helplessness nor the disparity between the numbers of the reapers and the quantity of the harvest (38). Do you see our twentieth-century world in these terms? Have you been called by name to be a labourer (1)? What work are you doing? Are you energetic? Are you praying (38)?

The messengers of the King 10:5–15

The over-riding feature of this section is the urgency of the message. Make a list of the points which lead to such a conclusion. There are at least five. Does the commission to the apostles apply to us today in its entirety? What principles in their strategy apply to us today? Are there any features which are purely local to this time and situation and which do not apply today? If our message is the same as theirs (7), how do we express it today? What are the modern equivalents for verses 13 and 14?

The servants of the King 10:16–25

The world is hostile to the King and his servants; if you don't believe it, you're a fool! What does it mean to be wise and innocent (16)? Answer the question, not from your own imagination, but from the passage (e.g. 19, 21–23, 25). What other scripture sheds light on it? The promise of the Spirit (20) is to destroy anxiety (21) and not the disciples' grasp on their message. It is sometimes used as an excuse for the failure to understand and prepare what we have to say, but Jesus had to learn the Scriptures, and so must we (24).

176

The place of prayer in Bible study

Photography is, among other things, the art of communicating through pictures. The photographer who is preoccupied with his camera, his lenses and his tripod has got things out of perspective. That can happen with Bible study also. We may be so conscious of techniques and details—and even with truth—that we forget that we are communicating with God. As you learn how to study the Bible, experience will soon teach you that prayer is a natural and indispensable part of searching the Scriptures. It is more than our line to God while he speaks to us through the passage. In prayer we see our own attitudes change as resistance melts and our hearts become open to the truth. But also prayer alters God's attitude toward us; 'When we confess our sins . . .' Prayer is more than psychological conditioning. It is the tangible way we express our faith in God. We are praying to him with assurance that he will take action. When we pray, 'Open my eyes, that I may behold wondrous things out of thy law,' we believe that God will show us new things from Scripture.

If you limit prayer to a quick preface, you are likely to miss a great experience. Who knows the answer when we come across a difficult or perplexing passage? God does! Ask him to make it clear or to help you accept what is already plain. You may see God open your mind in a way you would not have believed possible. If you read something which delights you or encourages you, thank God.

Bible study, if it is to be purposeful, should end with a prayer which asks God to help us take seriously our submission to his Word. 'What would you have me to do, or think, or avoid, or obey, or believe?' Even a clear answer to that isn't all that is required. We will then want to ask God for strength to do his will and for a persistent desire to grow into the likeness of Christ.

The requirements and rewards of the King
10 : 26–42

The news of the kingdom brings division (24–36) and we are required to follow the King before even our own family (37), losing our life in order to find it (39). Such conditions of service may well cause us to be afraid (26), but we know where the power lies (28–30). Secret discipleship is out (26, 27) and public identification essential (32, 33). But if the King demands a lot, he also gives a lot. What are the rewards (28, 31, 32, 39)? Look up the commentary on 41. In spite of distress when the kingdom comes, protection and provision are the lot of his subjects (29–31, 42).

The mystery of the kingdom

Identifying the King
11 : 1–19

From prison, John's evidence was only second-hand, and his predicted two-fold baptism of fire and water (3:11) didn't seem to have materialized. Jesus reassures him that Isaiah's prophecy is being fulfilled, and that though his sovereignty is not yet fully displayed, the signs of the beginning are there (4–6). But what of John himself? The greatest of all prophets was the least in the kingdom (11). Why? The illustration from the children's game is dramatic. Its import is that you can't have it both ways. You choose what you want to accept (14) and what you want to hear (15) at your peril.

The judgment and mercy of the King
11 : 20–30

This is a crucial passage in the light of the previous chapters which have highlighted the words and deeds of Jesus. The latter demand a reaction of a particular sort (20, 21). Benign indifference is not a viable option, and neither is simple amazement, for Jesus is no magician. His words and deeds betray a moral stature which demands our *repentance*. Is that your response in reading the account? For, be warned, you have seen and heard. And yet, if the judgment is real, so is the mercy. He is the one who reveals and refreshes (25, 28).

The King of the sabbath   12 : 1–14

It is not a question of Jesus' law versus the sabbath law, but of Jesus' interpretation versus the Pharisees' interpretation. What principle is he enunciating (3, 4) and on what basis (6, 8)? Clearly he is castigating their selective reading and application of Scripture in both stories (3, 5 and 11). What inconsistency does he find in their view of things? Both Jesus and the Pharisees have worked out their principles and their practice. The wrong principles of the Pharisees lead to wrong practice: the correct principles of Jesus lead to correct practice and bitter opposition (14).

The undivided kingdom   12 : 15–37

The first coming of the King is as a servant (18) and so his ministry is quiet and veiled (19). Compare his second coming (Matthew 24:29–31). The antagonism of the Pharisees is shown to be based on false logic; as Tasker puts it,' Civil war always has disastrous results.' Verse 29 beautifully describes the coming of the kingdom, for the strong man of the world (Satan) has been bound, though not completely, and the plunder has begun! The warnings in verses 30–32 are serious (see a commentary on the meaning of the sin against the Spirit). The immutable law of cause and effect applies in the spiritual realm as well as in agriculture (33–37).

The sign of the King   12 : 38–50

Substantial evidence of Jesus' identity had already been given, and in that light, sign-seeking was testimony to inner wickedness (39). A further sign, however, would be given for those with eyes to see (40). What does it mean? Contrast the preaching of Jonah and the preaching of Jesus. Can you locate passages which demonstrate the wisdom of Jesus? Verses 43–45 are a solemn warning. The departure of the unclean spirit (repentance) must be followed by the new Spirit's occupation if disastrous results are to be avoided. Not the whole of Jesus' generation was evil though (46–50). Some of them form his new family.

Parables of the kingdom

The insignificance of the kingdom 13 : 1–23

A word on interpreting parables: they are stories told in real-life settings in which not every detail has a spiritual counterpart. There is usually only one main point which is being driven home. What is it in this parable? The teaching of this parable is an amazing reversal of what was expected of the coming kingdom by Jews steeped in the Old Testament prophecies (see Daniel 2:31–45). They expected it would carry all before it. Jesus teaches that the kingdom *is* here, but not with irresistible power. It is hidden, not overt, and can be rejected. What ensures its reception?

The hidden nature of the kingdom 13 : 24–43

It's so easy to miss the point by concentrating on the details. Did you really get hold of yesterday's parable? If not, go back to it for a few days' study. In the first parable, it is a common misinterpretation to suggest the field is the church. Why is this wrong (38)? All three parables are about the *unexpected* character of the kingdom. What features can you identify? (To get you started—parable one is to scotch the idea that separation will occur now.) What encouragement and what warning does this teaching contain?

The value of the kingdom 13 : 44–58

Again, these parables are told to combat misconceptions. The treasure and the pearl are to confirm that the kingdom is the most valuable thing in the world, lest by its hidden nature and insignifcance we should be tempted to doubt it. It really is worth selling everything for it. Do you believe that? The dragnet is to confirm that, although the kingdom has come in an unexpected manner, it will issue in judgment and separation. Verse 52 contains a wonderful summary of the thrust of these parables. If you don't understand it, look it up in a commentary. Verses 53–58 are salutary. Take them to heart.

The community of the kingdom

The death of the forerunner 14:1–12

The Gospel is not written in strict chronological order. John's death had taken place earlier but Matthew records it here in the light of Herod's increasing concern about Jesus. It is a gruesome story which serves to remind us that servants of the King are not taken out of the context of real living. These were real characters whose nature we can identify in our contemporaries, and the story has a ring of truth about it. The death of Jesus took place in a human and political situation too. Compare them.

The provisions of the kingdom 14:13–36

Two very famous stories. All Scripture is recorded for our learning (can you recall the reference?). So what are we meant to learn from these accounts? Notice how beautifully gentle and yet how firm Jesus is (16) and how the disciples protest their inadequacy. It is not wrong to 'spiritualize' the story: there really is a spiritual analogy. In our world today there is a desperate shortage of spiritual food. What are you doing about it and how are you going about it? Don't bypass the practice of Jesus without applying it to yourself (23). What was Jesus trying to teach the disciples by walking on the water?

The ethics of the kingdom 15:1–20

In the light of the teaching of Jesus on either side of verse 7, define what a hypocrite is. Before we write off the Pharisees and scribes, let's recognize the high standard that Jesus sets (3, 6). It's not necessarily easy to identify where the Word of God ends and our tradition begins; to do so implies that you *know* the Word of God and that you have subjected your traditions to criticism. Do you and have you? What is the morality that matters (8–20)? Is there a divorce in your life (8)?

The wholeness of the kingdom 15 : 21–39

The site and object of these two miracles are very important. Jesus is in Gentile country with Gentile people (possibly in order to have more peace and quiet to teach his disciples), but his mission is limited to the Jews (24). His response to the woman is to wait for evidence of real faith (27), and then, in healing her, to give a glimpse that his kingdom will be wider than old Israel. Similarly with the healings (30, 31) and with the feeding of the four thousand. Why does Matthew include accounts of both feedings in his narrative?

The teaching of the kingdom 16 : 1–12

Notice that the Pharisees are joined by the Sadducees. Why would the sign of Jonah be particularly unacceptable to them (see Matthew 23:23)? Jesus is not condemning acute observation; indeed he is busy advocating it (3). What is he condemning (4)? Two strands of thought are interwoven in verses 5–12: (i) the need for faith in Christ's power (8–10), (ii) the need for caution with the teaching of the Pharisees and Sadducees. What were the characteristics of the teaching of the two parties? If you don't know, look it up.* Who are their modern equivalents? Are you wary of them?

The keys of the kingdom 16 : 13–28

Verse 17 stands as an abiding testimony that our perception of the King's identity is the work of God alone. How was Jesus different from the three proposed answers (14)? Verse 19 is the royal seal on the authority of Peter's subsequent life. He remained all too human (21–23), but, as the foundation of the church, his word to us (in his preaching in Acts and in his letters) is binding. The recognition in verse 17 has painful consequences (24), turning upside down our whole way of life (25). If only we could ask questions as shrewd as his (26)!

---

*B. M. Metzger, *The New Testament: its background, growth and content* (Lutterworth, 1970), pp. 40 ff.

The insiders of the kingdom
17 : 1–13

The transfiguration is the central event to reassure the disciples (7) that, in spite of all his apparent powerlessness in the weeks to come, Jesus is in fact the King. Moses represents the law and Elijah the prophets (3). What is their significance? Verse 5 wonderfully describes the call of the New Testament; it is *to listen*. This defines for all time what a disciple is—someone who listens and does what he is told. The story stands as a warning to us that reality may not always be what it seems to be.

The power and the weakness of the kingdom
17 : 14–27

Faith and power are related (19, 20)—a little faith brings a lot of power (20), but it takes time for us to learn our lessons (17). Verses 22 and 23 are in striking contrast to verse 20. Why? What does it tell us about Jesus' death—deliberate or accidental? We are not distressed, like the disciples (23), as we read the story because we know the reason for it and the outcome. Could you explain it to someone else? The incident with the tax collectors is recorded only in Matthew, and is full of allusion to Jesus' character and ministry.

Entry into the kingdom
18 : 1–14

The trouble with this incident is that it is too familiar to us. It conjures up a rather sentimental picture of childhood innocence. In fact it was a striking and shocking analogy because Jesus was highlighting a different feature of children. (What child is innocent anyway!) Which feature? Surely dependence. Nothing belongs to a child except what he is given; he can't buy anything, he must receive everything. And so it is with the kingdom. Verse 6 stands against those who think they can get in any other way. What drastic action have you taken (7–9)?

Behaviour in the kingdom   18:15–35

The kingdom is populated by those who know they are forgiven, and they must never forget it. What is the point of the progression from verse 15 to verse 17? Peter's question (21) betrays his minuscule thinking. The mark of the growing Christian is that he realizes that the debt which Christ has paid for him was much bigger than he originally thought (22, 24, 27). Forgiveness is the passport into the kingdom and the hallmark within the kingdom. An attractive characteristic, and a rare one! Are you practising kingdom ethics? Grudges are out. Meditate on the motivation for forgiveness.

The imminence of the kingdom

New laws for the new kingdom?   19:1–15

This is a difficult passage on a difficult question. Our approach to it is therefore all the more important. An invariable recipe for muddle and disaster is to look at the details first! So ask yourself first what are the main principles (4, 5, 8) and what conclusions are derived from these principles (6, 9). What is Jesus' attitude to the law and to the nature of man (6, 8)? Does belonging to the kingdom preclude marriage? (Careful how you answer! 10–12.) It is interesting that verses 13–15 should be placed next to a passage on divorce! The attitude of Jesus to children was revolutionary in his time.

Possessions and the kingdom   19:16–30

The man seems to think that one great act will gain entrance into the kingdom (16). How does Jesus answer that (17)? What is the significant omission in Jesus' reply (18, 19)? Some folk think that these verses teach a counsel of perfection for a spiritual elite. What features dissuade one from such a conclusion (21, 22, 23)? Kingdom teaching would be impossible without a supernatural God (26). Note first how the apostles share in the kingdom (28) and then how all his followers have a place (29), whether latecomers or not (30). Covetousness can keep you out of the kingdom, but poverty is no automatic passport (24).

The generosity of the King   20:1–16

This parable is recorded only in Matthew, and it is the subject of a plethora of interpretations (see commentaries). It requires hard work, not just a five-minute glance, if it is to yield its secret. It is told in reply to Peter's question (chapter 19:27) and its main point is the climactic verse 15 (not 16), a declaration of the sovereign grace and goodwill of God. It is *not* primarily about vocation, equality before God or the economics of employment. It is a sharp reminder that the King is free to do what he likes. Which other parables teach the same point?

Pecking-orders and the kingdom   20:17–34

This is the third prediction of the King's sufferings (17–19). Notice how Matthew significantly records it alongside the question of rank in the kingdom (20–28). What is the connection between the two? Greatness in the kingdom does not depend on ambition and authority, but on suffering and service (26, 27). Kingdom teaching often contains a reversal of our expectations. Can you list its unexpected features? The King is the Servant, not only in word but in deed too (29–34). It is those in need who recognize his origin (30, 31) and depend on his humility (32, 33).

The King comes   21:1–11

What a momentous event! You must get into it in your imagination, for there are a multitude of significant details. The king is coming to his city (what do you know about the significance of Jerusalem for the Jew?) but his entrance is not with the outward pomp of royalty (compare chapter 20:17–34). The air is thick with curiosity and expectation (10). They know his immediate origin (12), and some seem confident of his identity (9), but many no doubt were puzzled and not a few had hopes of political deliverance. Welcome (8, 9) and rejection (27:22, 23) are not far apart.

Making way for the kingdom 21 : 12–22

These two incidents have a common thread; in both, Jesus condemns a Jewish institution that has failed in its function: (i) the temple where the worship had become corrupt (13); (ii) the nation which had produced no fruit (19). The blind and the lame were excluded from the temple by the old purity laws (14) and to have shouting children was a scandal (15), but true religion is instinctively recognized by both groups. What does the kingdom drive out before it (12) and what results does its coming bring (13, 21, 22)?

What do you make of the kingdom? 21 : 23–32

The question (23) is an understandable one in the circumstances and one that has remained relevant in every age. Is the authority of Jesus genuine or bogus? His reply by putting another question is not evasive but typical of rabbinic debate, and their failure to answer (27) means that the initiative is his. The parable (28–31) is bluntly explained to them (31, 32) and the emphasis lies on the fact that action or lack of it betrays an attitude of heart and mind. What response demonstrates that we believe he is the King?

To whom the kingdom belongs 21 : 33–46

A pointed story indeed! But though it was understood by those to whom it was directed (45) its truth was too unpalatable (46). The parable is an allegory; identify the vineyard, the owner, the servants and the son. The common thread through the teaching is 'rejection'. Follow it through verses 35, 36, 37, 39, 41 and 42. Israel as a nation had so often been restored by God, but Jesus applies these verses from Psalm 118:22, 23 to himself. Where was he rejected; where was the foundation laid; what is the building being erected (42)? What is the fruit of the kingdom (43)?

The invitation of the kingdom 22 : 1–14

Wedding invitations are special; there has been extensive preparation by the host at great expense, and the wedding day itself is a day of joy and delight. To refuse the invitation(s) on any grounds, let alone those given in verse 5, is madness itself. But so it is with the kingdom; many of those invited don't see that it transcends all other considerations. And so it is the poor who recognize its value and accept (9, 10). What might the wedding garment refer to (11)? Do you see the balance between the doctrines of election and free will (3, 5, 14)?

Politics and the kingdom 22 : 15–46

Jesus' reply to the Pharisees could occupy a lifetime of study (15–22). It is the basis of all Christian teaching on the relationship between church and state. Christians belong to two kingdoms; we owe conditional loyalty to the state and unconditional loyalty to God (21). Jesus is not primarily a political liberator (compare John 18:33–38). Don't ask trick questions of Jesus (23, 35), for it only demonstrates your ignorance (29). It is he who does the questioning (41–46); it is his prerogative as King. He will ask you about resurrection (28), about the commandments (40) and about himself (42). What do you know?

The enemies of the kingdom 23 : 1–22

This is the last public discourse which Matthew records, and it may well parallel Deuteronomy 32: 1–43, Jesus being the second Moses (2). In what ways does the kingdom teaching differ from the teaching and practice of the Pharisees? That is a difficult question but it is worth working at it and writing down your answer. Note how Jesus not only castigates them (4–7, 13–15, 16–18) but gives telling explanations of their error (8–12, 19–22). It is fatally easy to be an enemy of the kingdom, making rules for others which you don't obey yourself and neglecting the kingdom rules where they hurt.

Problem passages

The more deeply we know the Bible, the more conscious we become of some of the moral and intellectual problems it seems to present. These include apparent internal disagreements, inexplicable events, and approval of patent evil. How do we approach them?

Problems of understanding

As always the main need is to know more accurately what the Bible is saying when translated accurately, set in context, and seen in historical perspective. Elisha's she-bears are not lashing out at a childish prank but judging a deliberate pagan insult to God; Jesus' teaching on divorce fits together against the current debate of the day; and the two Palm Sunday asses in Matthew may be circumstantial detail, or may point to the fulfilment of Scripture. On passages which we really cannot understand we should have the humility not to pass judgment ignorantly.

Problems of belief

Here we must be sure what the Bible is asking us to believe; it does not expect us to read poetry as science, nor to claim as supernatural an event with a natural explanation. But it does ask us to look beyond mere science to the hand of God in the timing and shaping of events, and especially to acknowledge the unique (and experimentally unrepeatable) circumstances created by the presence of God's own Son on earth. This applies to Moses at the sea as well as Jesus' powers over nature, food and health, not to mention his own resurrection or ascension. We need also to ask what our motives are for wanting not to believe; is it real puzzlement, or fear of the challenge?

Problems of morality

Evil deeds recorded in the Bible are there as warnings, not examples. Much is also explained if it is set in historical context: 'an eye for an eye' asserted strict justice in preference to vendetta. We should beware of our own inconsistency; we can hardly criticize God for not calling evil to account and then blame him for doing just that in judgment and hell.

Realities in the kingdom 23 : 23–39

Life in the kingdom involves proportion—neither obsession nor neglect (23, 24), consistency—both inside and outside (25–28), and contemporaneity—applying history and not merely judging it (29–31). These strong words get to the root of things; it takes effort to apply them to your own life and situation. Jesus spoke plainly about hell (33); it is an uncomfortable theme study that you should do. How do you interpret verses 34–36? To use Tasker's comment on Jesus' lament (37–39), it is 'the truth spoken in love'. The King stands in mercy now (37); one day he will come in judgment (39).

The coming of the kingdom 24 : 1–14

Two comings in judgment are interwoven here—the destruction of the temple and the second coming of Jesus (see commentaries). The teaching of Jesus about his kingdom indicates that it has both present and future aspects; it was inaugurated at his first coming and will be completed at his second. 'The church age is the period of Christ's concealed glory' (Ladd). In this interim period Satan has great power for deception (4, 5), for destruction (6, 7), and for persecution (9–12). The best sign for the imminent return of the King is verse 14; we are near that point.

The rise of false kings 24 : 15–28

This is theological 'tiger country', with a multitude of interpretations and a wealth of commentary. Whichever 'days' are referred to, we know that they will be urgent (17, 18) and unpleasant (19–21). They will be characterized by falsity (23–26), and Jesus' warning is clear and unmistakable (25). To be forewarned is to be forearmed. The end will be swift and universal (27); it is certain and inevitable (27, 28). The whole realm of apocalyptic literature and eschatological teaching is a fascinating and important one.

For further reading: Leon Morris, *Apocalyptic* (IVP, 1973); W. J. Grier, *The momentous event* (Banner of Truth, 1970).

The delay of the kingdom 24 : 29–51

Again, this is a much debated passage. Could verses 30 and 31 refer to the preaching of the gospel, when the Son's power and glory are seen (30) and the elect gathered (31)? What are the other interpretations? The next section teaches patience (33–34) and confidence (35) while verses 36–51 are an exhortation to vigilance, for though the delay of the King's return may seem interminable, with everything going on as usual (38–41), it will happen suddenly and unexpectedly (42–44). Its timing is unpredictable; its inevitability is undoubted by the faithful and wise (45–51). How does readiness show itself (46)?

Preparation for the kingdom 25 : 1–13

One of the most striking features of Jesus' teaching is the urgency of it, and it is worth tracing that theme through Matthew's Gospel. The force of this passage is inescapable: '*Now* is the day of salvation.' There will come a day when it will be too late (10), when repentance will be of no avail (9) and neglect of the things of the kingdom will be past rectifying. It is a truly terrible picture of exclusion from the King's wedding feast, based not so much on whether we know him but on whether he knows us (12). Are you telling others to prepare and watch (13)?

Investment for the kingdom 25 : 14–30

These 'parousia parables' were designed to wake up a sleepy people to the seriousness of the times. The King's absence implies responsible stewardship from his servants (14) who will be called to account on his return (19–30), and what they do with his generous gifts and opportunities will betray their attitude to him (20, 22, 24, 25). Note that responsibility and blessing increase together and faithfulness is rewarded by both (21, 23, 29). This kingdom teaching needs to be worked out in practice, both by individuals and within the context of the church.

190

Inheriting the kingdom   25 : 31–46
The striking thing about this parable is that both groups were
surprised at the verdict; the righteous were only doing what
they thought was natural and obvious (37–39), and the unrighteous didn't realize that real religion involved practicalities
(44, 45). Discipleship means a changed life. The three stories in
this chapter hang together. The Christian life is a busy one (no
sleep, 5; no hiding, 25; no sloth, 35). It is also a balanced one: it
has an inner dimension (prepared lamps, 1–13) and an outer
dimension (hard work, 14–46). It has a spiritual side and a
practical side, a love for Christ and a love for our neighbour.

The royal road

The King's preparation   26 : 1–16
We begin here the most significant journey in the world's
history—the royal road. The events happen quickly (1, 2), with
human intrigue and cunning (3–5), and treachery that forms
the most awful sale of all time (14–16). In the middle of all this,
there is an act of astonishing insight (6–13) which speaks
volumes of commentary on the coming events. In what ways
does the woman's action highlight his impending death? There
are numerous points of contrast and comparison, *e.g.* the cost
of the sacrifice, the scepticism about its value, *etc.* (What
others can you find?) What do you make of verse 13?

The King's betrayal   26 : 17–25
God's timing is always perfect (18); the fact that it was
passover is no accident. What do you know about the
passover? (Read the account in Exodus 12.) How does the
passover parallel the supreme sacrifice of Jesus? God's ways
are always perfect, using even betrayal to forward his purposes
(*cf.* Genesis 37). Enemies of the kingdom are to be found
amongst his closest followers (23); the disciples' form of
address ('Lord') and that of Judas ('Master') both convey
respect and honour. Loyalty and treachery may not be far apart,
but the King knows the difference (25).

191

The King's meal   26 : 26–35

They had probably had passover meals together before, but
this one was to be special. It was special because he invested it,
not with magical powers, but with significance (26–28). It was
an ordinary meal symbolizing an extraordinary fact (28), with
bread and wine as vivid testimonies to his sacrificial death.
Today, this supper is to be celebrated 'to proclaim his death until he comes' (1 Corinthians 2:26); the cross is to be proclaimed
as his throne until he comes as King. The meal anticipates an
even closer fellowship (29). The intimacy of the meal, however,
is no formula for faithfulness (30–35).

The King's cup   26 : 36–46

Peter and the others profess to be willing to die with him (35),
but they cannot even pray with him (40, 43, 45). It has often
been pointed out that, at decisive moments in his life, Jesus
spent particular time in prayer. What other occasion can you
remember? 'The cup (39) is an Old Testament metaphor used
of punishment and retribution' (Hill). What does that tell us of
the purpose of his death? The fact that the royal road is not easy
travelling for the King is an encouragement to his followers in
their travels. What lessons do we learn from his prayer (39, 42,
44)?

The King's arrest   26 : 47–56

The irony in this scene is breathtaking—the King of kings with
supreme authority and power (53) is met with swords and
clubs (47); the one whose affection for his world knows no
bounds is betrayed by a kiss (49); the teacher whose work is not
done in a corner is taken under cover of night (20). The kingdom
was not to be extended by the use of arms (51, 52). Ought verse
52, however, to be used as an argument for a pacifist position?
Note how Jesus was not ignorant of or disobedient to the
Scriptures (54).

The King's testimony 26 : 57–68

False testimony is needed to condemn the King of truth (59), but agreement is not easily come by (60). Little did Caiaphas and the Sanhedrin realize their part in the fulfilment of Jesus' words (61; see John 2 : 19). It seems that they recognized them as a messianic claim, which prompts their question under oath (63). Jesus' testimony is brief but unequivocal (64). What time does he refer to in verse 64? Meditate on the charge—blasphemy, and the phrase 'He deserves death'. What is the significance of these details? It is true to say that he was self-condemned?

The King's follower 26 : 69–75

This is one of the most poignant stories in Scripture. What are the precursors of denial (58)? This verse gives two valuable clues, one to do with method and one to do with motive. The progression (69–74) is all too easily visualized, with small beginnings (70) leading to an awful crescendo (74); from a mild attempt at ignorance to outright vehemence. How characteristically human! Our small denials will lead to big ones; pray that the cock crows early for you and that your response is like Peter's (75), for God can use such material (Matthew 16 : 18; Acts 2 : 14).

The King's price 27 : 1–10

The King is innocent (4); his betrayer is guilty (3). The King dies voluntarily bearing the guilt of the world; his betrayer takes his own life bearing his own guilt (5). The price for the King's death is thirty pieces of silver—that buys freedom for the world! It buys, not a burial place for strangers (7), but forgiveness and friendship with God! Presumably the money came from the treasury in the first place (6); how true to form that it should be happily used for betrayal and yet be considered defiled on its return!

The King's humiliation 27 : 11–31

We follow a King who has suffered much—mentally (his abandonment by the disciples, his denial by Peter, his betrayal by Judas) and physically (a long series of trials, a scourging, a gruelling game). Similar treatment may well await those who follow him today, being seemingly pawns in a political game, with friends in unexpected places (19) but whose influence does not match crowd pressure (23). The whole story, however, breathes divine permission and divine significance. What scriptural basis is there for viewing Christ's death as a substitution?

The King's salvation 27 : 32–44

And so the King of history stands at the crossroads of history—a grim but glorious place (33). He, the Lord of men, is at the mercy of men (35, 36); he, the giver, dies with the robbers (38); he, the one who saves others (42), does not save himself. The charges are correct (37) and the saying is true and to be fulfilled (40), but note how people are looking for the wrong evidence (40, 42). To such his sovereignty is veiled and his authority is hidden. He is master of the situation, however, for his trust is in the Father, not for deliverance (43) but in obedience.

The King's triumph 27 : 45–54

Others had borne such physical and mental agony; no-one has borne such spiritual agony (46). We can understand his suffering at the hands of men, but how do we explain his suffering at the hands of God? Peter writes later with breathtaking simplicity that it was the innocent (1 Peter 1:19, 2:22; 3:18) dying in place of the guilty (1 Peter 2:24, 3:18). Look up the Old Testament references on the temple curtain; its tearing symbolizes our free access into God's presence. The cross is not a tragedy or a mistake. It looks like a defeat for the King; it is in fact his defeat of the enemy, disarming death (52, 53).

The King's security   27 : 55–66

What an extraordinary time to declare your allegiance to the King! The leader is dead (58–60), the disciples have disappeared except for a few brave women (61) and the cause is apparently finished—then Joseph commits himself (57)! Did he have an inkling of what was to happen? Did he understand that the cross was to be the King's throne? We shall never know, but it reminds us that the eleventh hour is not too late. Jesus is always a security risk (62–66) and because his kingship is no fraud (63) he doesn't need the disciples' help (64).

The King's appearance   28 : 1–15

The King has no authority until he has won a power base. This he has done (6)! Verse 6 contains the most important negative in the world, for the tomb's emptiness is of paramount importance. We may remain sceptical about visions, but the absence of the body is unaccountable, requiring specious stories from those who find the facts embarrassing (11–15). His appearance, however, is important too—the King has not *disappeared* but has *reappeared* (7, 10). Why is it important? Why did the appearances stop? What is the significance of his appearing in Galilee?

The King's commission   28 : 16–20

The doubters (17) need to examine the evidence (John 20:27), as well as their own motives for ignoring or rejecting him. Worship springs out of the facts (17). The King's authority is all-powerful (18) and all-embracing (19). There is no question of power sharing. He has the right to command absolute obedience from all; his servants have no option but to 'go' and no duty but to baptize and teach (baptism, the King's seal; teaching, the King's commandments). All this is impossible without his presence. He has promised that all who go out to proclaim him will keep his presence (28).

6. Problems of church life

The New Testament consistently presents the ordinary local church as the place where God is. There he is worshipped, there he is at work; there the life-style of Christ is to be seen among his people. Tragically, there is a massive credibility gap between the Bible's vision and so many local Christian groups we know; everything from lurid scandals and great rifts of heresy to piffling squabbles over status, cash and furniture have spoilt the picture. Yet the Bible, too, is a realistic book; its authors write to real situations, offering earthy but profound solutions.

These studies merely touch on the main problems and remedies. We offer only a few guidelines to your study, leaving you to explore the passages given (and others) and come to your own conclusions. In every case you need to ask: how does this problem arise, and how do we remedy it? Keep in mind your own experience of church life, and let it challenge any over-easy answers.

Division

1 Corinthians 1; 3:1–9; 6:1–8
Psalm 133
Ephesians 4
Matthew 18
James 3:1—4:12

Unity among God's people has proved elusive ever since the disciples fought over who would be the greatest. But is 'church unity' at the large, organizational level the same kind of thing as unity among individuals at the local level? Which is easier to work for—and which is more important? Can we have unity without uniformity?

How do factors like doctrinal disagreement, personality clashes and cultural variations interact in causing division? Should we seek unity at any price—and if not, what can justify our holding back?

Error
1 Corinthians 1:20–25; 2; 3; 4; 15:1–11
Psalm 119
Colossians 1; 2
John 8:12–59
2 Peter 1:1—2:3

Where does wrong belief come from?

The Bible underlines the link between knowing the truth and living it out. How many of the pressures towards heresy have moral rather than intellectual roots?

Dig out the Bible's teaching on truth as connected with God, with Jesus, and with the Holy Spirit. What does this say about reducing truth to mere propositions? Find out what is meant by 'mystery' and 'fullness' in Colossians. Whose job is it to preserve Christian truth in the local church?

Stagnation
1 Corinthians 3:1–3; 4:8–21; 14
1 Kings 10; 11
Hebrews 4:14—6:12
Luke 9:51–62; 14:25–35
Revelation 2; 3

Many things seem to slow up Christian growth. What is the role of (i) self-confidence, (ii) laziness, (iii) sin, (iv) indifference, (v) fatigue? What are the remedies? Can familiarity breed contempt, even of Christ?

What is the relationship between individual and corporate growth? Individualism cramps the growth of a fellowship; can the reverse be true too?

Suppose you are trying to help the development of a newer Christian than yourself; what would you try to offer in the way of doctrinal understanding, moral challenge and practical wisdom? How would you attempt to motivate him?

Immorality
1 Corinthians 5; 6:9–20
Isaiah 5
1 John 3
2 Corinthians 6:1—7:1
John 15–17
Colossians 3

Why is immoral behaviour inconsistent with Christian faith? What forms can it take? How does a slack attitude undermine our own relationship with God, and our credibility with others?

There is a clear demand for Christian distinctiveness, but this should not mean isolation from society. What does it mean to be 'in the world but not of it'? How can one be holy but not holier-than-thou?

Christians have different views about borderline issues, and the boundaries of Christian freedom. What do these includes, and how should we approach them? (See Legalism, p. 199.)

Ineffectiveness
1 Corinthians 2:1–5; 5:9–13; 12
Ezekiel 1–3
Ephesians 6:10–24
2 Corinthians 10; 12
John 14
1 Peter 3:8—4:19

Christians often appear to make a great deal of noise to little effect. How far is this due to (i) lack of contact with God, (ii) lack of contact with people, (iii) lack of co-operation with each other?

Is it true that any effective church provokes opposition? Peter advises Christians facing human opposition, while Paul alerts us to spiritual enemies; how should we face these two? How does prayer relate to effective witness—and how can we take it seriously without retreating further into cliques?

Role confusion
1 Corinthians 7; 14:26–36
Proverbs 30; 31
Ephesians 5:21—6:9
Matthew 19:1–15
Titus

Two issues overlap here: the structures of relationship which God intended, and the manner in which relationships should be conducted. The principles of mutual consideration, respect and responsibility apply whether the roles are those of husband and wife, child and parent, single and married, employer and employee or church member and elder.

God's intended structures are not always so easy to see. How permanent was the stress on remaining single or the subordinate role of women meant to be? Are there equal and opposite pitfalls to avoid? List what you think *is* clear.

Legalism
1 Corinthians 6:9–20; 8; 10:14–33
1 Samuel 21:1–6
Romans 14:1—15:13
Matthew 7:1–5; 12:1–14
Galatians

Some Christian standards are fixed; others can vary with personal conscience or cultural change. When the flexible becomes fixed, that is legalism.

In Corinth, meat from pagan worship was sometimes offered to Christians. Some people said meat was meat, but others thought any link with paganism compromised their loyalty to Christ.

Selfish legalism can operate in two ways: to expand my freedom despite others' feelings, or to limit everyone to my blinkered view. What are the principles? How do they apply to dress, drinking alcohol, or the use of Sunday?

Leadership
1 Corinthians 1; 3; 9
Exodus 18
John 13
2 Corinthians 1; 2; 4; 7; 11; 12
Mark 10:32—45
1 Peter 5
(Other main passages on leadership are of course 1 and 2 Timothy and Titus. See pp. 129, 163.)

What are the main features of Paul's example as a Christian leader? How can such confidence co-exist with humility?

In many churches the leadership is in the hands of too few people; they become over-busy and constitute a bottleneck. What is the Bible's antidote to this? How can we find more leaders?

What are the personal attributes which qualify a person for Christian leadership? What things should mark the leader's attitude to those he leads?

Short-sightedness
1 Corinthians 10; 15
Isaiah 6
1 Thessalonians 4
2 Corinthians 5
John 1: 1—34
Revelation 20—22

The Christian walks by faith, not by sight; but he tends to slip into seeing things from this life's perspective, and not as God has revealed them to be. How does the New Testament combat this danger in its teaching on (i) Christ's incarnation, (ii) the resurrection, (iii) heaven, hell and judgment, and (iv) Christ's return and the future of the world?

Paul says, 'From now on we regard no one from a human point of view.' What does this mean, and how should it affect our attitudes and approach to people?

Muddle
1 Corinthians 11; 12; 14
Ezekiel 40; 43; 47
Ephesians 5:1–20
Matthew 6:1–8
Hebrews 8:1—10:25

Public worship can be a shambles or a deadly formal business.
The Bible envisages neither; even Ezekiel's vision of a renewed
Jerusalem combines orderly structure with the flowing water
of life. Its distinguishing feature is the presence of the living
God, who banishes disorder and dry ritualism equally. What are
the differences between Jewish and Christian worship
highlighted in Hebrews?

How does Paul envisage each individual making his contribution? How would it work in your local fellowship? What is
the antidote to domination by a few, whether paid ministers or
others?

Lovelessness
1 Corinthians 6:1–8; 13; 16
2 Kings 4
James 2
2 Corinthians 8; 9
Luke 8:19–56
1 John

How does love show itself in the lives of Elisha, Jesus and Paul?
One could argue that some of Paul's ideas (for example on
litigation or fund-raising) are quite inapplicable in our complex
society. Is this true? Is our failure to love others a matter of our
attitude towards them, or is it simply that we fail to work out our
love in practical terms? The Bible's picture of love is quite con-
crete: what specific areas could be listed for action in your own
life, your home, your work, your church?

Testing error

Many of our contemporaries don't believe in truth and therefore are not worried about error. But as disciples of the Lord Jesus, we claim that there is truth, and, as a consequence, error. The trouble is knowing which is which, and it matters because if we are wrong it could cost us or others dearly. God always tells the whole truth, but Satan rarely tells an outright lie; he mixes truth with just enough falsehood to distort it all. How does error, or heresy, come about?

1 Some people *deny the truthfulness* of the Bible. In practice they ignore its plain teaching and will not be corrected even if one shows them plainly from the Bible that they and God disagree. Such people have not submitted their *minds* to the lordship of Christ.

2 Some *add to* the Bible, giving to recent writings the stature of the Word of God. Such cults as Mormonism and Christian Science claim to believe Scripture, but in practice demonstrate that they think it incomplete. By showing them contradictions between the Bible and their own writings you may help them to see that if God is consistent their own writings must be spurious. Some churches give the church itself a place of authority equal with the Scriptures, and in that way include in their teachings things which may not be true.

3 Some stand on the complete trustworthiness of the Bible and yet disagree with each other in some matters. This includes recognized heretics like Jehovah's Witnesses and also Christians who differ over fine points. Here we must dig out what the whole Bible really teaches, noting the prominence it gives the issue, and paying attention to what Christians have understood in the past.

In the search for truth we rely on the Holy Spirit, yet that in itself has sometimes become the supposed source of wrong teaching. The Holy Spirit will only declare to us the things of Christ, and we can automatically reject anything which contradicts Scripture or fails to give Jesus pre-eminence.

7. The Bible and the mature Christian

Perhaps it's a bit early to say, as Hebrews does, 'By this time you ought to be teachers', but by now you must have some idea of what is in the Bible, and some idea of how to study it for yourself. Listed below are some aspects of what the Bible becomes to the mature Christian. With these as seed thoughts, can you plan and follow some studies for each one, finding appropriate passages for yourself? What further aspects would you like to add? How far has the Bible become these things for you already?

The Bible: an aid to worship
a yardstick for truth
a portrait of God
a handbook for family life
a daily reminder
a spur to evangelism
an aid to growth
a source of power
a light to your path
a commission to responsible living
a window into reality

O God, keep your Bible fresh to me for life; let me grow in knowledge, in obedience to Christ, and in usefulness on earth.

V
How to write menus

Part of the aim of this book has been to work itself out of a job. The hope is that you will be able to study your Bible, and devise plans for studying it, without the prop of *Food for life.*

In practice, the way to do this is to keep your eyes open for ideas of things you want to study and for helpful aids. Keep a list of subjects to explore, and plan them in some kind of order: set yourself aims for this week, this month, and the next six months. Know your church or CU bookstall and the local Christian bookshop, and get hold of the aids you need. Sometimes you will feel like leaning back on someone else's printed plan; at other times you will want to use your initiative and dig the material out of your concordance, commentaries, *etc.* A loose-leaf notebook or folder can hold your planning as well as the growing record of your studies. Keep it in some kind of order so that you can use the material for talks or group studies when you need it.

For your own good we are going to stop here and leave you to work it out for yourself.

Bon appetit!

Index of Bible passages

208